Getting to GPS
Grips with

Mastering the Skills of GPS Navigation and Digital Mapping

Peter Judd
Simon Brown

 cordee Published by **Cordee**,
3a De Montfort Street, Leicester, LE1 7HD, Great Britain

First edition: 2006

Published by Cordee Ltd,
3a de Montfort Street, Leicester LE1 7HD, England
www.cordee.co.uk

Printed by Fratelli Spada SpA, Rome

ISBN 1904207 38 3

A catalogue record for this book is available from the
British Library

Design, typesetting and production
by **Vertebrate Graphics Ltd**

Vertebrate   www.v-graphics.co.uk
Graphics

The contents of this book were believed to be correct at the
time of printing. Nevertheless, the authors, the publishers
and their agents cannot be held responsible for any errors or
omissions, or for changes in the details given in this book, or
for the consequences of any reliance on the information it
provides. This does not affect your statutory rights. We have
made every effort to ensure the accuracy of this guide but
technology is always advancing, so we welcome any feedback
readers may have. E-mail your comments to info@cordee.co.uk.

Ordnance Survey®
www.ordnancesurvey.co.uk

Picture Credits
Val Corbett; Outdoor Training & Leisure Ltd; Evo Distribution
Ltd; Magellan Inc; Garmin Ltd; Ordnance Survey; Navman (NZ)
Ltd; Mike Billing, Northport Systems Inc; Anquet Technology
Ltd; Sir Chris Bonington CBE.

Getting to GPS
Grips with

Mastering the Skills of GPS Navigation and Digital Mapping

Peter Judd
Simon Brown

CONTENTS

Foreword ix
Introduction x
Acknowledgements xii
Health and Safety xii

01 Traditional navigation and GPS use 1
Introduction 2
 Paper Maps 3
 Grid Systems 3
 Compass Use 5
 Awareness of your surroundings
 as an aid to navigation 6
 Pacing and Distance 6

02 GPS Explained 9
Introduction 10
GPS Systems 10
 Satellite Based Augmentation
 Systems (SBAS) 10
How the GPS System Works 11
 GPS and Augmentation Systems 12
 Reception and errors 13
 Antennae 14
Making Your Choice 16
 The Main Manufacturers of Handheld GPS .. 17
 The Features of Different GPS Systems 18
 GPS Building Blocks 20
Mapping GPS and Related Software 21
 Mapping GPS – the difference 21
 Colour Screen 22
 Street Mapping 22
 Topographical Mapping 23
Buying the Right GPS for Your Needs 24
 Buying Online 24
 Buying on the High Street 25
 Future-proofing 25
You're Not on Your Own! 26
 GPS Manufacturers' Websites
 and Support Services 26
 Frequently Asked Questions (FAQs) 28

User Forums 28
Training Products, Training Courses
and other support 29
GPS Training Courses 30
Try out the latest GPS before you buy 31

03 First Steps.. **33**
Introduction 34
    Power Up 34
    Default 34
    Keys/buttons 34
Main Pages 36
Setting up your GPS....................... 42
Navigational Data 54
    Factory Input Data 54
    User-Created Data 54
GPS Features and Functions................ 59
    The Mark function 59
    Landmarks/Waypoints/
    Points of Interest (POI) 60
    The GoTo Function 62
    Routes................................ 63
    The Track Function 64

04 Step-by-Step User Guide **67**
Introduction 68
Step-by-step diagrams of the features
and functions of **Garmin GPS** 69
Step-by-step diagrams of the features
and functions of **Magellan GPS** 82

05 Digital Maps Explained **97**
Introduction 98
Digital Mapping Software 98
What Types of Digital Maps are Available? 100
    Land-based maps 100
    Street Maps........................... 101
    Marine Charts........................ 102
    Aviation Charts....................... 102
    Worldwide Digital Maps 103
Which Software Do You Buy? 103
    Narrowing the choice 105

The Main Suppliers of Mapping Software
in the UK 106
    Anquet Technology 106
    Memory-Map 106
    Fugawi 107
    Tracklogs 107
Getting Started and Connecting to your PC 108
    Getting Started 108
    Connecting to your PC 109
    Types of connections 110

06 **Bringing it all together** 113
Introduction 114
Route Planning Basics with Paper Maps 114
    Putting together a Route Plan 115
    Waypoints in a Route 117
    Navigating a Route 117
    Traditional Route Planning Reviewed 118
Route Planning with a
Digital Mapping System 118
    Save and Share your Routes and Tracks 119
    Save As Screen 121
Route Planning with a Digital Mapping
System and a GPS 121
    Waypoint Placement with a GPS 122
    Tips on route planning with GPS in mind .. 124
    Getting the best out of the
    Route function 124
Be Prepared Before You Set Off 128
    Batteries 128
    Before leaving home 128
    Before moving off 129
    On the walk 129
    On arrival at a waypoint in a route 129
    On arrival at your destination
    (or on a GoTo) 129
    Staying Safe with your GPS 131
    Use the latest GPS software 131

07 **More Uses for your GPS** 139
Using your GPS Abroad 140
Making GPS Fun 144
    Ready Prepared GPS Routes 144

Geocaching and Geotrailing 146
Additional Partners for your
GPS and Digital Maps 150
    PDAs and Pocket PCs 150
    GPS links 151
    Where and what to buy? 152
Auto Navigation Software 154
    In-car Systems 154
    PDA/Integrated GPS and
    Auto Navigation Software 154
    Handheld Colour Mapping GPS
    and Auto Navigation Software 155
What Does the Future Hold for GPS? 156

Appendices 159
Glossary 160
Answers to "Check your Learning" Questions .. 165
25 Questions to ask yourself 166
GPS Checklist 168
User GPS Checklist 169
Index 170
Index of Diagrams 176

Foreword

Once again GPS Training has come up with the goods.
Users of Global Positioning Systems have been looking
for an easy to understand guide focussed on the issues
of GPS navigation in the United Kingdom. This is it!

I found the excellent colour images and the easy to
understand step-by-step instructions most interesting.
Coupled with clear and easy to read explanations,
it provides a complete guide to how this technology
works. I am sure it will help you get the best from
your GPS.

I would have no hesitation in recommending this
publication, as I feel sure it will provide you with
the tools required to master GPS navigation.

Sir Chris Bonington CBE

Introduction

We have written this book because there are very few publications available for the GPS user. Those that have been written seem to be mostly highly technical, academic or focussed on another country. It is our belief that there is a real need for an easy to read guide so that people can get the best from the GPS or mapping system they have bought or are thinking of buying.

Unbiased advice is invaluable and we have tried to provide that in this guide. However this is a market dominated by a small number of national and international players. In some segments choice is limited, with certain suppliers being the clear market leaders.

Peter Judd

Simon Brown

When a brand has a clear market lead there are usually good technical reasons. In some cases however it can be that the company is just more professional in its marketing approach. This in itself could still be a good reason to buy into that brand, as it is much more likely to stand the test of time and stay compatible with other linked products. The issue of compatibility is most important with this type of technology.

We have tried to give you options wherever possible, but ultimately you will have to make you own decisions based on the information you have to hand. We have tried to keep things simple and, where there are technical issues which do need some explanation, we have tried to keep this to a minimum. If we use terms that you don't fully understand, do look for them in the *Glossary* on page 160.

Our experience of running courses for many hundreds of people, is that once someone has grasped the basics and learned how to enter data into one type of GPS, then switching to another model or brand is relatively easy. Most of the information contained in this guide will apply to almost any GPS or mapping system.

The world of GPS has its own terminology so you will find a glossary at the end of the book which will give a brief explanation of these terms. Key learning points are highlighted and we have given you opportunities to check your learning along the way by answering questions or undertaking tasks.

The step-by-step guides showing GPS screens are based on the **Garmin eTrex C** range and the **Magellan eXplorist** range. However as the basic functions are similar on most other GPS, you should find them a useful guide whatever your GPS.

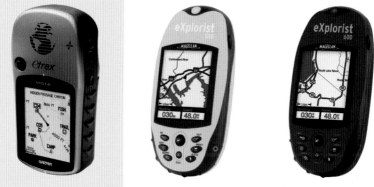

Garmin eTrex Vista C

Magellan eXplorist 500, 600

We hope you find this book useful and that it helps you become a safer and more confident GPS user, whether it's walking, biking, geocaching or whatever your outdoor sport.

Don't feel you are alone if you find that you still need help to master these systems. If all else fails, come and get some 'hands on' help on one of our training courses.

Enjoy using your GPS.

Peter Judd   *Simon Brown*

www.gpstraining.co.uk

Acknowledgements

Without the help of a number of people, this book would never have made it to the presses. They know who they are and our thanks go to all of them.

In particular we would like to thank Val Corbett for the use of some her excellent photos, and our Step by Step guides would not have been possible without the kind assistance and permissions from Matt Palmer of **Garmin** and Mark Wilhoft of **Magellan**.

We thank all our loyal customers, some of whom have ended up in the book, for their continued enthusiastic support.

Lastly we would like to thank our long-suffering wives – Jean and Tricia – without whose support and patience this book would never have been completed.

Health and Safety

Although we can accept no responsibility for your safety as you undertake any exercise or task suggested in this book, it is imperative you understand how easy it is to become so engrossed in what is happening on the GPS screen that hazards in the environment are not noticed. For your safety, please follow these simple guidelines:

- Please remember that your safety whenever you are outdoors is in your hands.
- Please take great care at all times.
- Please stay aware of what is going on around you – look and listen.
- Please do not take any unnecessary risks. Turn back if you feel unsafe.

01

Traditional navigation & GPS use

It is vital to have a basic working knowledge of traditional navigation to be able to use a GPS properly.

Introduction

As this guide is intended to be about GPS and digital maps we have had to assume that you have at least a working knowledge of traditional navigation. We will give you some pointers here that explain those aspects that are most important to the GPS user but if you feel you would like more information then we recommend ways you can improve your traditional navigation skills at the end of the chapter.

Below: Section of O.S. 1:50,000 Landranger Map and **bottom** 1:25,000 Explorer Map

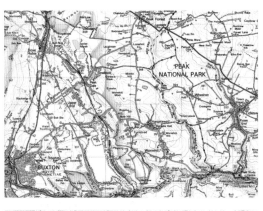

Paper Maps

Until recently there were just traditional printed maps. Now there are digital versions so we will refer to them as 'paper maps' and 'digital maps' to avoid confusion.

Crown Copyright protects the Ordnance Survey (OS) maps we use in the UK. More information about OS maps is available on their website www.ordnancesurvey.co.uk. The site contains comprehensive information for young and old alike, with particular attention to the educational needs of those wishing to learn more about maps and navigation. The most widely used OS paper maps are: Explorer Maps 1:25,000 scale (or 4cm to 1km) and Landranger Maps 1:50.000 scale (or 2cm to 1km).

These maps contain rights of way information for England, Wales and Scotland, selected places of interest and much more. The maps all contain a list of map symbols called the map legend.

Grid Systems

We use a grid system as a basis for calculating a position, for measuring distance, and to give the direction of grid north for taking compass bearings. Grids are the squares created by drawing horizontal and vertical lines on a map. In the OS grid system letters (for example, **NY**) identify large area grids, with the lines that divide them up into smaller grids being given identifying numbers. By using a combination of these letters and numbers we can identify a location on a map to a certain degree of accuracy.

Together, these letters and numbers are known as co-ordinates. By sub-dividing a grid we can narrow down the size of the square to give a more accurate position.

The Main Grid Systems

Understanding international map systems can be complicated, which is why most GPS receivers are designed to switch to other systems at the touch of a button. As not all map systems use grids, they are called map position formats. In most cases all you have to do is select the position format you wish to use and your unit will give you a position fix in that format.

Some popular map position formats include:
- Universal Transverse Mercator (UTM);
- latitude/longitude;
- British Grid (OSGB) – *see diagram overleaf.*

Most GPS receivers contain many more.

Here in the UK we are fortunate in having a very user-friendly map position format coupled with great mapping. We almost exclusively use the British Grid.

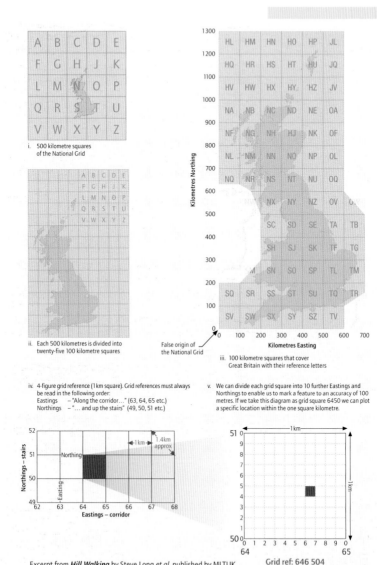

i. 500 kilometre squares of the National Grid

ii. Each 500 kilometres is divided into twenty-five 100 kilometre squares

False origin of the National Grid

Kilometres Northing

Kilometres Easting

iii. 100 kilometre squares that cover Great Britain with their reference letters

iv. 4-figure grid reference (1 km square). Grid references must always be read in the following order:
Eastings – "Along the corridor…" (63, 64, 65 etc.)
Northings – "… and up the stairs" (49, 50, 51 etc.)

v. We can divide each grid square into 10 further Eastings and Northings to enable us to mark a feature to an accuracy of 100 metres. If we take this diagram as grid square 6450 we can plot a specific location within the one square kilometre.

Northings – stairs

Northing

Easting

Eastings – corridor

Grid ref: 646 504

Excerpt from *Hill Walking* by Steve Long *et al*, published by MLTUK

Above: The British Grid System

Above: The Navigation Workshop DVD

Below: Using a Romer Scale

Compass Use

Being able to create a compass bearing is a basic navigational skill that everyone can easily achieve with the minimum of practise. If you need to brush up on your basic navigation then try either *Navigation for Walkers* by Julian Tippett published by *Cordee*, or for a more visual approach try *Memory-Map/GPS Training's Navigation Workshop* DVD. Both should be available from good outdoor stores.

Bearings and Headings

A GPS can display both but there is a subtle difference between the two. A bearing is a straight line compass direction to your destination usually expressed in degrees, whilst a heading is simply your current direction of travel also expressed in degrees. To be 'on course' your bearing and heading must be the same.

The Romer Scale

This is a 'must have' for all map users. A Romer scale can be found on some models of compass or can be bought as a separate piece of kit for less than a couple of pounds. To use it, place the point of the Romer on the location you wish to produce a grid reference for and read off the horizontal and vertical scales from the map to produce the co-ordinates.

expert tip

If methods of traditional navigation are new to you, you would benefit from a specially tailored one-day navigation course with GPS in mind – 'A Traditional Navigation Day'. Check out details on www.gpstraining.co.uk.

Left: Tony Warren – the GPS guru!

Awareness of your surroundings as an aid to navigation

Few people are aware of the wealth of information available to them in the map they carry. Many outdoor enthusiasts, orienteers and experienced mapreaders navigate purely by their maps. As they progress, they are aware of what is around them – for example, a stream on the left, a fence on the right, the ground rising on the left and the barn at the wall corner about 10m away – so they can be assured they are at the footbridge. The more you use this method of map reading the easier it will become. Eventually you could find yourself being much more aware of the landmarks that are all around you confirming your position on the ground and on the map.

Pacing and Distance

The average person takes 60 to 70 double paces to travel 100m over flat ground. You can use the GPS' distance recorder, called the odometer, to help you practise estimating distance. How many paces do you take?

T A S K :

Choose any interesting one-kilometre square on any 1:25,000 paper map. Using this square and the map legend, see how many different map symbols are used within this square.

Example: Using *OS Explorer OL5* we have found 19 different map symbols in the map square NY 36/30

Above: Checking a GPS grid reference against the map

CHECK YOUR LEARNING

1. **Who owns the copyright on all maps in the UK?**
   a) The Queen
   b) Ordnance Survey
   c) The Government

2. **Which direction do the vertical lines on a map point?**
   a) Grid north
   b) True north
   c) Magnetic north

3. **What is the correct GPS setting for position format for the UK?**
   a) UTM
   b) WGS 84
   c) OSGB

4. **Which grid reference do you read first when locating a position on a map?**
   a) northings
   b) eastings
   c) westings

5. **What is your current direction of travel?**
   a) Your bearing
   b) Your heading
   c) Your course

6. **How many double paces does the average person take in 100m?**
   a) 80–90
   b) 60–70
   c) 50–60

The answers can be found on page 165.

Left: Consulting the map before setting off

T A S K :

This task will help you to gain confidence in using your map to confirm your position as you progress along your route.

Establish where you are on the map then study your route ahead for the next 500m. (About half a grid square).

Make a mental note of the position of several features you will pass that you will easily recognise on the ground – for example, a footbridge you will go over in 200m (about 130 double paces away on average), a path joining yours from the left 200m after the bridge (another 130 double paces away) and then a farm you will pass about 65 double paces after the junction.

You can now put your map away for 500m and set off for the farm knowing that you will pass the footbridge and then the path junction on the way, confirming you are on course. You will know when each feature should come up by counting your paces. In this way you are moving from one known position to another. If for example the bridge does not appear after about 130 double paces you will be aware that you may have gone wrong somewhere and if necessary go back to a known position.

On arrival at the farm, you can confirm you are at the correct place by consulting your map. You can then repeat the process for the next 500m and so on.

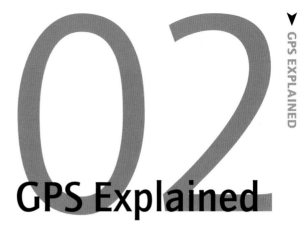

GPS Explained

GPS navigation is a wonderful example of how satellite technology can be harnessed to help the human race. This technology is already used by many sectors of industry, transport and support services to make our lives run more smoothly.

Introduction

A handheld GPS can be an excellent addition to an outdoor user's navigation system. It gives a position fix in any type of weather including hill fog. This service is totally free apart from batteries. This section includes what you need to know to start getting the best from your GPS. If you don't own a GPS yet, it will help you buy the best one for your needs.

GPS Systems

The global positioning satellite system (GPSS) was developed during the 'cold war' by the US military as a way of improving the accuracy of American intercontinental ballistic missiles.

As the US government wished to keep its military advantage, it deliberately degraded the GPS signal for civilian use so that accuracy varied widely. This system, called selective availability, was removed in May 2000 to give an average accuracy of 15m.

In theory, selective availability could be reinstated at any time but in practise the world is so dependent on this technology, it is very unlikely to happen.

Satellite Based Augmentation Systems (SBAS)

These systems are designed to improve the accuracy of GPSS by a factor of around five. Typically, they can produce a position fix down to 3m (10ft) horizontal and 6m (20ft) vertical.

They work by using stationary satellites and ground-based relay stations to improve the quality of the signal from the GPSS. Because it is a system based on fixed positions it has limited coverage. For example, we cannot get reliable US augmentation signals (their system is called WAAS) in Europe. For this reason, we have had to build our own system called EGNOS – the European Geostationary Navigation Overlay Service.

Significant dates in the evolution of GPSS:

1995 – the US GPS system becomes fully operational.

2000 – US selective availability was removed.

2007 – the Russian GLONASS system (another GPSS) scheduled to become operational.

2010 – the European GALILEO (our own GPSS) is scheduled to become operational.

How the GPS System Works

- GPSS uses a system of satellites (the US system uses 24) 11,000 miles above us circling the globe at around 1,000 miles per hour sending radio signals back to earth.
- Usually at least 6 satellites are visible at any one time.
- A GPS receiver can log on to 12–14 satellites simultaneously.
- A GPS needs to log on to at least 4 satellites and, by sharing a combination of distance, time and position information between the satellites, gives the user a fix of latitude, longitude and elevation. This is called a 3D fix.
- GPS firmware then turns the received information into usable displays.
- The GPS updates its position every second.
- Once you have bought your GPS, there is no charge for using the system.

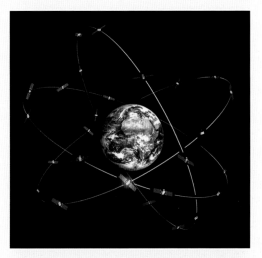

Images courtesy European Space Agency

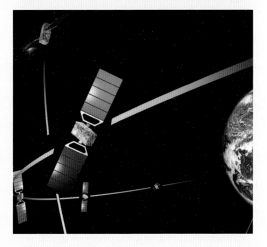

There is another system being developed to cover the Asia/Pacific area called MSAS. When these three systems are fully operational, most of the world will be able to receive these upgraded signals. Providing your GPS is WAAS compatible, it will be able to log onto these improved signals.

GPS and Augmentation Systems

Not all GPS are able to pick up these more accurate signals. If one does it will be called a 'WAAS or EGNOS compatible' GPS. This should be shown in the GPS' specifications and on the box. If it doesn't say this, it will not be compatible. Non-compatible GPS cannot be upgraded later.

Accuracy

A GPS gives you a position fix that theoretically puts you into a one square metre box on the ground. However, you should take the current accuracy reading of your GPS into account as well before you interpret this.

When taken together, the position fix and the accuracy reading will place you somewhere inside a circle of accuracy. The size of the circle of accuracy can change regularly as it depends on: how many satellites you are logged on to; where they are in the sky relative to you and to each other and the type of terrain you are in.

The typical accuracy of a GPS is 95% reliable and depends on what type it is:

- **Non WAAS-enabled GPS**
  Horizontal accuracy = 15m (49ft), placing you within a 30m circle
  Vertical accuracy = 19m (62ft) without an electronic barometer

- **WAAS-enabled GPS (5 times more accurate)**
  Horizontal accuracy = 3m (10ft), placing you within a 6m circle
  Vertical accuracy = 4m (12ft) without an electronic barometer

Your GPS will only place you reliably somewhere within the circle of accuracy.

e x p e r t   t i p

If you buy a non-WAAS/ EGNOS compatible GPS you will never be able to harness these new augmentation systems.

e x p e r t   t i p

You should always consult your map, especially in poor visibility or in dangerous terrain, to see what hazards exist within or near the circle of accuracy.

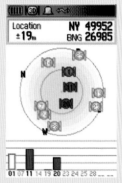

Above: A GPS showing current position as a British National Grid ten-digit reference

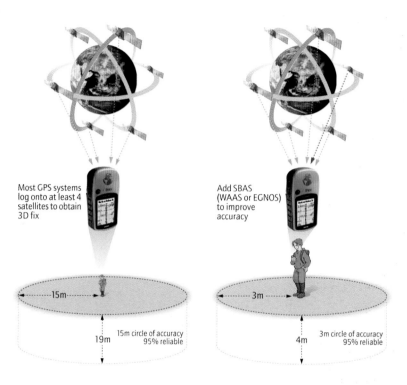

Most GPS systems log onto at least 4 satellites to obtain 3D fix

Add SBAS (WAAS or EGNOS) to improve accuracy

15m

3m

19m   15m circle of accuracy
95% reliable

4m   3m circle of accuracy
95% reliable

Reception and errors

The whole system relies on a good line of sight to the satellites: the stronger the signal, the more accurate will be the position fix. Reception is unaffected by bad weather. Reception can be affected or blocked by:

- tree cover, gullies, buildings, your body and other objects;
- poor position grouping of the satellites;
- reflected signals called multipaths;
- ionospheric distortion.

A 2D fix leaves out elevation and is less accurate than a 3D fix.

False Signals

Occasionally your GPS may receive a false signal and therefore give a false position and/or speed. This can be caused by poor satellite geometry. If all the satellites within your GPS' line of site are clustered closely together or are situated in a line away from the GPS antenna, the calculations necessary for establishing your position become more difficult and therefore less reliable.

Multipath Error
Here your GPS receives two signals from the same satellite, one being the true signal and the other being a reflected signal such as from rocky terrain, especially in gullies or from a building. These can cause an incorrect position fix to be given.

Ionospheric error
Atmospheric distortion, often caused by periods of high solar activity, can alter the speed of the satellite signal through the ionosphere. If your GPS starts doing strange things when receiving a poor signal always question your position, check your map and if necessary, move to a location where you can get a clear view of the sky and re-establish a good signal before proceeding.

Antennae
There are two types of GPS aerial – quadrifilar helix and patch. A quadrifilar helix aerial is a more sensitive instrument. Generally it will get a signal in conditions where a patch aerial will not.

Getting the best position fix:

If you want to be as certain as possible of your position, perhaps to mark it so you can return later, you need to follow these simple rules:

- make sure you have a 3D position fix;
- give your GPS time to settle in a stationary position and you will find that the accuracy or 'estimated position error' (EPE) improves;
- some GPS have an 'averaging' function to give the best possible position fix.

If you move a substantial distance from the last time you used your GPS, it will take longer to give a 3D position.

Far left: GPS with quadrifilar helix aerial
Left: GPS with patch aerial

CHECK YOUR LEARNING

1. How much does it cost to use the GPS System?
   a) £100 per annum
   b) It's free apart from batteries
   c) You are billed on how much you use it (like a mobile phone).

2. What is the average accuracy of GPS signals without WAAS or EGNOS?
   a) 50m
   b) 30m
   c) 15m

3. By what factor will EGNOS increase the accuracy of GPS signals?
   a) 10
   b) 5
   c) 2

4. How many satellites does a GPS need to log onto to obtain a 3D fix?
   a) 12
   b) 8
   c) 4

5. How often does a GPS update its position?
   a) Every hour
   b) Every minute
   c) Every second

The answers can be found on page 165.

Making Your Choice

The GPS market is still developing rapidly, but for the outdoor user it is already dominated by two multi-nationals, US-based Garmin – the market leader – with Magellan, some way behind but catching up. Satellite Based Augmentation Systems that improve accuracy down to 3m, coupled with the recent development of quality digital mapping software, have provided a catalyst for considerable growth in the handheld GPS market segment.

With sales of handheld GPS virtually doubling each year, prices are now becoming very affordable. Sales of GPS should grow to a point where it is likely that most outdoor users will possess one. However, it is the combination of GPS and digital maps that will drive the market in the future.

It is difficult to choose the best global positioning system for your needs if you don't understand the differences between the models and don't know the right questions to ask. Here we are going to give you the basic information you need to start making an informed choice.

Many people buy a GPS based on a perception of their needs but with no real idea of the potential of these systems. The most important piece of advice we can give is to find out what they can do before you buy, and where your end use fits in within the multitude of different models and software combinations.

With prices ranging from under a £100 to over £400, mistakes can be costly, so some research before you buy could save money, time and frustration in the long term. Our experience is that when users find out what a GPS can really do, and discover how easy it is to connect the system to digital mapping software, they tend to change their ideas on which features are important to them.

Your GPS *will* allow you to:

- see your position as a grid reference – this is updated every second;
- record your movements across the ground as you travel (a track log);
- mark your current position at any time;
- input the grid reference of any position at any time;
- save waypoints to a database for future use;
- navigate on a dynamic straight line bearing to a given location;
- add waypoints together to make routes and create a database of them;
- navigate a route as a series of straight line bearings between waypoints;
- see on the map screen where you are in relation to waypoints and your route;
- plan and enter escape routes;
- view waypoint information as you navigate, such as current position, speed and time as well as current distance from the next waypoint and the time it will take you get there at your current speed;

Your GPS *will* allow you to: (continued)

- create and navigate a reversed route or track;
- set an audible proximity alarm (if it has this feature);
- download and upload waypoints, routes and marks between your GPS and PC, laptop or PDA if you have digital mapping software system or a waypoint management system – this is dependent on your GPS model;
- download and upload points of interest and street level mapping if you buy the extra software needed – this feature is only possible with certain models of GPS.
- join more than 750,000 people worldwide who take part in the growing sport of geocaching.

Make sure you purchase the correct model for your use both now and in the future by ensuring you have all the information at your fingertips before you part with your cash. You will find a buying checklist on page 168 that will tell you what features we think are essential and desirable, and then let you fill out your own checklist to produce a profile of your ideal GPS. You can use this as a 'crib sheet' to take with you on your GPS shopping expedition so that you can weigh up the models against your checklist.

Before you buy, you need to know what a GPS will and won't do. Here are two lists that set out in fairly non-technical way what the average entry level GPS is and is not capable of. We have tried to minimise the use of GPS jargon, however some terms are unavoidable. If you need to clarify the meaning of a particular term just use the glossary.

The Main Manufacturers of Handheld GPS

Garmin and **Magellan** are the two most significant players in the market place with the other manufacturers taking a fairly small share between them. Whether this is healthy for the trade is difficult to say. The manufacture of GPS receivers is at the leading edge of technology, with vast sums being set aside for product development. Small wonder then that few companies have the resources to invest in this type of product.

Whilst the manufacturers have been innovative, most systems deliver the same functions with variation in presentation. Once you have grasped the principle of how one system works, it's fairly easy to switch between different systems.

Some of the greatest steps forward have been taken in the area of complementary software systems. This is what has fired the imagination of the GPS user, driving the market forward. Who knows what the next innovation will be? This is an issue we cover later in the book.

The Features of Different GPS Systems

Each manufacturer produces a number of ranges and models all aimed at different segments of the market. So how do we sort these out into some sort of order that makes sense to us? The trade splits up the ranges and places each model into a category based around the technical level of the features included and, to some degree, the expected end use of the prospective user.

There is quite a sizeable market out there for GPS at a basic level where being able to communicate with a PC is not required and navigation will be at the most elementary. This is the starting point for most ranges. From here on, like most things in life, the more whistles and bells you add the more things cost. GPS is no different.

There are no hard and fast rules as to where any one model fits in to the following categories other than common sense:

- **Entry Level GPS** – should at the very least be able to perform most of the tasks described previously in the *Your GPS will allow you to* list on page 16, with the exception of downloading mapping software and all software related functions. Some models may not be able to link to a PC in which case all data will have to be entered by hand through the keyboard.
- **Mapping GPS** – used to describe a model that will include all the features of an entry level GPS. It will be able to connect to a PC and have sufficient memory to allow downloads of compatible software solutions. It may or may not have a colour screen, electronic compass or barometric altimeter, all of which will be price dependent. The features of mapping GPS are explained in more detail on page 21.
- **Component GPS** – covers pretty well anything that doesn't fit into the other categories. This includes devices such as PDAs that have integrated GPS, PDAs that link by wire or wireless technology to GPS and GPS-enabled mobile phones.

Your GPS *will not*:

- ever be a permanent substitute for a map and compass;
- work properly unless it has been set up correctly;
- work without batteries;
- provide a navigational bearing unless you have 'told' it where you want to go;
- be as accurate when it does not have clear view of the sky, such as indoors, in narrow gullies or under tree cover;
- be as accurate when ionospheric or multipath errors occur;
- give you a correct compass orientation or bearing until you start moving, unless you have a GPS with an electronic compass;
- place you at a precise location. It will only put you within a circle of accuracy. The size of the circle depends on the type of terrain, the number of satellites you are logged onto, and their position relative to you and each other. The type of GPS you are using will be a factor too.

ENTRY-LEVEL GPS

Garmin entry-level GPS systems

Magellan entry-level GPS systems

MAPPING GPS

Garmin mapping GPS systems

Magellan mapping GPS systems

COMPONENT GPS

Navman component GPS systems

Pocket PC with integrated GPS

GPS Building Blocks

Think of 'features' as the building blocks a GPS is made from, some of which are essential, the rest desirable or not on your shopping list. Obviously the more features and the more memory in-built into the package the more costly the model will be. You can find a checklist to help you make a decision about what you need from a GPS on page 168.

At this stage some of these terms and ideas might seem to be 'double dutch' to you. Don't worry as we will be explaining what all these features do and their importance in the GPS scheme of things. If anything is not clear, please refer to the *Glossary* on page 160.

With all this information you will probably know more about GPS than many sales assistants in the average outdoor store. We hope you will use that knowledge to get a good deal and, most importantly, the best GPS for your needs.

T A S K :

If you haven't bought a GPS yet, use our checklists at the back of the book to ensure you choose the right GPS for your needs.

If you already have a GPS, use the same checklist to see if it is still the right model for your current and future needs.

The main GPS features to consider are as follows:

- WAAS enabled;
- database for waypoints;
- capacity to store more than one route and track;
- exchanges data between the GPS and PC;
- good quality colour screen;
- database of points of interest;
- memory to store extra points of interest and street mapping;
- electronic compass and barometric altimeter;
- elevation profile on screen;
- audible proximity alarm;
- waterproof to IPX7 standard;
- cable, case and lanyard included;
- USB cable included or RS232/USB converter cable available at a reasonable price;
- downloadable firmware upgrades.

Mapping GPS and Related Software

Having mastered the basics and discovered the powerful combination of GPS and digital mapping it is no wonder that the user is turning to the mapping GPS as a means of getting more software solutions into a handheld receiver. For a relatively small number of bucks you can now achieve a pretty big bang.

A mapping GPS cannot display maps in all their glory, but every new software development is taking a step closer to achieving the ultimate dream – good quality topographical mapping displayed on a colour screen on a robust and waterproof handheld receiver.

Lower cost memory and software is creating a boom in the market allowing decent chunks of street and topographical maps, and more recently, turn-by-turn navigation software to be downloaded to the handheld receiver. They bring some pretty sophisticated software solutions within the budget of most users.

Mapping GPS – the difference

An entry level GPS is not designed to work with maps. It has a much smaller memory, a lower resolution screen and cannot be upgraded. Some models will however show the location of some larger cities on the map/plot screen. A mapping GPS will contain more memory than an entry level GPS, typically from 8Mb to 115Mb. The bigger the memory, the bigger the tile or chunk of map you can download to your GPS. It will have a higher resolution screen, probably colour with typically 16 to 256 colours. There will be a factory loaded base map of some sort that shows basic infrastructure such as main roads, railways, rivers, lakes and so on.

It will have the ability to communicate with a PC and download portions of specialist digital mapping supplied only by the GPS manufacturer into the receiver's memory. The obvious limitation to the size of the download is the size of the GPS' in-built memory. The capacity of a GPS' memory cannot be increased unless it is a model that uses removable memory cards. With this type there is often an increase in cost, but the reward is far greater flexibility. This trend is likely to develop as GPS manufacturers adopt digital camera memory techniques.

At the present time it is not possible to see the full detail of a 1:25,000 scale map on the screen, purely because the memory and screen size available would limit the amount of information available to the user. The solution is to use a cut down map – see *Topographical Mapping* on page 23.

Colour Screen

Colour screens for mapping GPS are now available with differing levels of display quality. If you want to buy a GPS to use with street or topographical mapping and take advantage of the recent developments in software, then our advice is to buy a model with a good quality colour screen. There is an enormous difference between the screen quality of product offerings so ask to see mapping shown on the screen of the GPS before you purchase.

Street Mapping

A mapping GPS will accept downloads of specialist detailed street maps and points of interest (attractions, restaurants, garages and so on) supplied only by the GPS manufacturer up to its memory capability. Some versions of these maps allow the user to find an address and then navigate to it with turn-by-turn directions. These maps are not part of a digital mapping system such as *Memory-Map* (*see page 106*). They are sold separately as CDs and usually cover large land masses (Europe, for example).

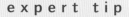

expert tip

If you have doubts about spending that little extra for a colour screen, then ask yourself, when was the last time you saw anyone using a PC with a black and white screen?

Above: Black and white (*left*) and colour (*right*) screens

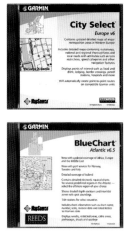

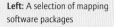

Left: A selection of mapping software packages

Right: Auto Navigation Kit designed for use with a handheld GPS

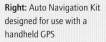

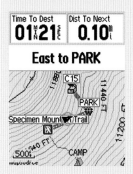

Above: MapSend Topo as seen on eXplorist 500

Topographical Mapping

Mapping GPS made by some manufacturers have a stripped down version of a digital topographical map available for purchase on a CD. This provides a very basic sort of map on the screen with limited contour lines and features being shown. They are not available for every country. Do look at these maps before you buy to make sure that you understand what they will look like on your GPS screen.

As the GPS manufacturer or their licensed agents produce all GPS mapping products, they are usually only compatible with mapping models produced by that same manufacturer.

Right: Topographical mapping as seen on the Garmin 60CS

Buying the Right GPS for Your Needs

How and where should I buy? There are a bewildering number of retailers out there all looking for your business, whether they are your local outdoor store, a multiple or one of the new breed of e-tailers. Our advice is to make them work hard for your money.

Buying Online

Buying from the Internet can be impersonal, but if you are looking just for the best price then this could be the way to go. Internet retailers usually have easy to use websites with good buying advice and some will set up the GPS for you. On the whole they give good value for money but cannot offer personal face-to-face service. If you buy from abroad, make sure the GPS has a European basemap (if it is a mapping model).

- **Remember** – you may know more than the average shop assistant. Check how much s/he really knows about GPS before accepting their advice.
- Make sure you are able to handle the product.
- Ensure it is a working model – look at the screen quality and ease of use.
- Ask for a demonstration of both GPS and mapping software.
- Make sure the salesperson understands your needs.
- If recommended an alternative GPS, question why.
- If you decide to buy, ask for your GPS to be set up for you before you actually purchase it. If the shop cannot do this for you, don't buy from them.
- Ask what happens if you have a problem post purchase.
- Don't be afraid to ask for some sort of deal. For example, ask for batteries and/or cables to be included.

Right: Helping a customer make the right GPS choice

Remember you may have to pay duty and tax when importing it.

The downside of buying online is you can't see and handle the GPS before buying.

Buying on the High Street

Most good outdoor retailers will stock GPS and mapping software. The advantage here is you can handle the goods before purchase and usually receive helpful product information from well-trained staff. Some stores will be able to demonstrate a mapping system on an in-store display. After sales service should be more accessible.

The downside of buying on the high street is that it is not always the cheapest. Shop around for the best deal.

Future-proofing

Our final piece of advice on this subject is, with so many new products and software solutions on the market to choose from, to think of your future needs when you do make that all-important decision. You would be surprised at the number of people who attend our courses with their own GPS who wish they had had our advice before they bought. Fortunately for them we do offer a part exchange scheme.

If you have made an expensive mistake and bought a GPS that isn't right for you, or just fancy moving up to something with the latest colour features, then why not consider an exchange?

GPS Training will consider an exchange deal on most modern GPS, as we can either use them on our training days or offer them as a low cost GPS unit to our clients at our courses.

We will make you a fair offer for your GPS (provided it meets our criteria) and put together an attractive package for you on the GPS of your choice.

You're Not on Your Own!

There is a lot of information available to users who wish to know more about a product such as specifications, performance details, or simply 'how to' questions. By its nature a lot of this information will be of a technical nature which is guaranteed to put many of us off.

Whilst some users find the owner's manual an adequate resource for acquiring GPS skills, a significant number don't appear to and, from the experience of talking to participants on our training courses, many never get beyond a position fix. In many cases their GPS just gets shoved to the back of a drawer and forgotten.

Below we point you towards assistance offered by the manufacturers and software houses, as well as give you alternative options for learning how to get the best from your GPS and mapping system.

GPS Manufacturers' Websites and Support Services
These are a good source of information, especially technical information. These websites provide prospective purchasers with detailed specifications and information about the products and services they have to offer, as well as unlock facilities for software.

We have listed some useful manufacturer information below:

Garmin
www.garmin.com   **Telephone: 01794 519944**
Outdoor products are shown at: www.garmin.com/outdoor
A low or high-resolution video is available of the main features of a Garmin GPS that can be downloaded from the specific product page. Garmin have extensive support, product information, a very good FAQ page and a software upgrade facility on the Internet.

Magellan
www.magellangps.com   **Telephone: 0800 62435526**
Outdoor products are shown at: www.magellangps.com/en/gpsAdventures/outdoor/
Magellan outdoor products information is available online, including full product specifications and downloadable images. There is useful information for geocachers, as well as details of available software and product support.

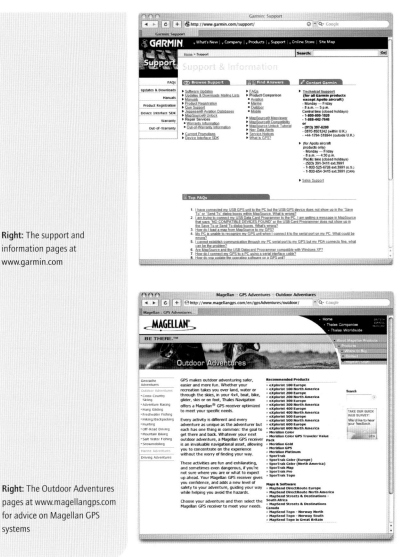

Right: The support and information pages at www.garmin.com

Right: The Outdoor Adventures pages at www.magellangps.com for advice on Magellan GPS systems

Although we do not have the space to list all the manufacturers of GPS receivers, two others are worth looking at.

Lowrance   www.lowrance.com

Based in Oklahoma, Lowrance produces a range of GPS that are becoming available in the UK. In the USA it has a well-deserved reputation amongst the marine fraternity.

Silva   www.silva.se

Silva is a Swedish company renowned not only for its compasses, but also for GPS, altimeters and technical watches. Their Multi-Navigator GPS had a high reputation in military circles. More recently Silva is making available a new range of GPS which no doubt will continue their reputation in this field.

Frequently Asked Questions (FAQs)

Most manufacturers and software houses have pages on their websites dedicated to FAQs. They can be helpful if you are stuck and need an answer to a fairly standard type of question but they can tend to be a bit technical. The lists of questions are generally based on the most frequently asked questions received by the technical support teams and are of course aimed at cutting down the number of customer calls made to them.

User Forums

These are website-based and allow members to exchange information on subjects relating to GPS. They can be a very useful way to get answers to questions you would not find on the manufacturers' websites.

There are several useful forums on the Internet, including: www.globalpositioningsystems.co.uk, www.pocketgps.co.uk and www.gpspassion.com.

Training Products, Training Courses and other support

Our experience is that many users lack the patience to read manuals and approach the whole subject with trepidation thinking that the technical aspects of GPS technology will be beyond them.

It doesn't help that there are so many different models to choose from in a highly competitive market. Added to that, these products are widely available from all over the world through the Internet. It's small wonder that many consumers feel they need guidance and training not only to purchase the best system for their needs but also to get the best from their GPS.

Below: OK – What's next?
A GPS Training day

Manufacturers do their best to provide manuals and guidance online for their customers, but like any other producer of technical goods it is not within their remit to train the user to use the product. We know from our own experience that there is a growing demand for quality GPS training.

We believe that the manufacturers and the retail trade have been slow to realise the importance of training not only for their staff but also for the consumer. Apart from a few enlightened retailers, few staff in outdoor shops know enough about the product to properly help and advise their customers to make an informed purchase. We do know that many early purchasers of GPS received poor advice leading to them buying a model that didn't always suit their end use. This is now changing and both manufacturers and retailers are making great efforts to improve training for their staff. They are supporting us in our efforts to provide training for both consumer and retail staff alike.

There are several ways to obtain the information you need to use GPS in the great outdoors:

- **Magazines:** A good source of information can be outdoor magazines. They have realised the importance of GPS and mapping software to the mainstream recreational user. They now have regular features and reviews of the latest products, as well as access to walk routes that can be downloaded into your GPS (these are called pre-coded walks) and geotrails.

TRAINING PRODUCTS, TRAINING COURSES AND OTHER SUPPORT

- **Video: Garmin** in particular have produced several product-specific videos. They are relatively brief but can be quite helpful in explaining the basics in a visual way.

- **Navigation Workshop DVD:** The DVD that *Memory-Map* has produced in partnership with *GPS Training* is a useful and highly innovative training product. This is a simple-to-use interactive DVD that is both visual and intuitive. It provides a step-by-step guide to using maps, compass and a GPS. You can learn to plan routes and brush up your map reading skills as well as getting the most from your GPS. As co-producers of the DVD, we are proud that the DVD has been endorsed by mountaineering legend Sir Chris Bonington.

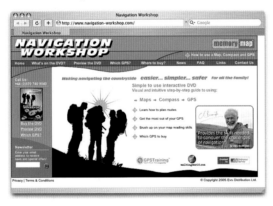

Left: The Navigation Workshop website

The DVD is supported by its own website www.navigation-workshop.com where you can preview the product and find links to compatible manufacturer's information on which GPS to buy.

GPS Training Courses

We specialise in GPS, digital map and traditional map and compass navigation training for anyone whose sport takes them into the great outdoors. We have an excellent range of courses on offer designed for every level of navigation experience.

We are proud to be approved training partners by all the market leaders – **Garmin**®, **Magellan**®, **Memory-Map**™ and **Silva**®.

Above: A GPS training group
Above centre: A typical navigation day
Above right: GPS training in the field

Right: The GPS Training courses page, giving advice about the training courses available

Try out the latest GPS before you buy

If you haven't invested in a GPS yet, we recommend you don't buy until you've been on one of our courses. During the course we will help you decide on the GPS that's best for your needs and for your budget. On the course, you can choose to try out a GPS that might fit the bill from our wide range of current models.

Our courses run from lovely locations with walking usually available straight out the door. Plans are underway to make our training courses available nationwide as we find suitable partners and locations. Whatever your training needs, there will be a course that's right for you. Start at that point and progress from there. Full information on all our courses is provided on our website www.gpstraining.co.uk as well as a secure online booking facility.

First Steps

This chapter explores the menus, buried sub-menus and commands that make your GPS work. It may seem a bit complicated at first, but with some practise, you will soon feel comfortable with the buttons and functions of your unit.

Introduction

In this chapter, we will cover how to power up the GPS, we will then explain the buttons, show how the main menu works and describe how sub-menus fit in. Next we will deal with how to set up the GPS to work correctly and lastly we will show how the various navigation screens present information and, in addition, go through how the GPS database should be used.

GPS setup diagrams can be found on the following pages:

Garmin GPS – page 43
Magellan GPS – page 50

Power Up
This simply means to switch on the GPS. Use the instructions in your manual to insert the correct batteries the right way round and press, and hold in, the power button until the screen comes up. Some GPS will require you to press the **Enter** key after switching on to confirm you want to stay switched on whilst others need you to press the **Page** key a few times to get past the loading pages.

Default
When you first take your GPS out of the box, your GPS will be set to 'default' or preset factory settings. A GPS will not work correctly on default hence the need to set it up for use at your current location.

Keys/buttons
Most GPS have buttons that cover the following functions:
- **PAGE** to move from one page to another until you get back to your starting page;
- **ENTER** to confirm that this is what you want to do;
- **FIND** to find stored waypoints and points of interest;
- **QUIT** to cancel what you are trying to do;
- **GOTO** to navigate to a single already stored waypoint;
- **MENU** to access the main menu of the GPS;
- **MARK** to capture the current position so that it can be stored, amended or navigated to;
- **IN/OUT** to zoom in and out on the map/plot page;
- **SCROLL** some form of scrolling device – a four-way button or 5-way click stick.

Explaining the Keys

Garmin GPS

1 Zoom In/Zoom Out
Whilst viewing the map screen, press to zoom the map view in and out. Look at scale on screen.

On any other page use these keys to scroll up and down a list or to move a slider bar.

2 Find/Options
Press and hold to show the waypoint find menu.

Press and release to show the options menu for a page.

3 Thumb Stick
(a four way scrolling device and **Enter** button)
The GPS is designed to be used in the left hand with the thumb stick being operated with the thumb.

Press down and release to select highlighted options or data or to confirm on-screen messages.

Push up/down/left/right to move through lists, highlight areas, buttons or icons or to move the map panning arrow on the map screen.

4 Page/Quit/Compass On/Off
Press and release to cycle through the screen pages.

This button can also be used to 'quit' a process when working within a page.

Press and hold in to toggle the electronic compass on and off (**Vista C** only).

5 Power/Backlight
Press and hold in to switch on and off. When GPS is on, press and release to switch on and adjust backlighting, view the date and time, satellite and battery status. Move slider bar on screen to adjust brightness.

$\geqslant$ **GARMIN**

Magellan GPS

1 Backlight
Press & release to turn on the display backlight. Press and hold to adjust the intensity of the backlight.

2 Zoom In
Whilst viewing the map screen, press to zoom the map view in. Look at scale on screen.

3 Nav
Press to show each navigation screen in sequence – Map; Compass; Position; Satellite.

4 Mark
This button saves your current position as a point of interest. These are stored in the *My Points of Interest* section of the database.

5 Power
Press the button and hold in to switch on and off. When the startup screen is shown, press the **Enter** button to confirm.

6 Esc
If pressed, this cancels the current action then cycles backwards through the navigation screens.

7 Arrow Joystick/Enter
Push up/down/left/right to scroll through lists or position the cursor on the map screen.

Press down to confirm an action or select a highlighted menu item or button.

8 Zoom Out
Whilst viewing the map screen, press to zoom the map view out. Look at scale on screen.

9 Menu
Press and release to show a menu with available options listed.

10 GoTo
This creates a one leg route from your current position to a point of interest selected from the database or by pointing to a location on the map screen.

Main Pages

Whilst you are navigating you will be able to see a lot of information about your journey on different screens. Although these are similar, each manufacturer chooses to display this information in slightly different ways. **Garmin** call these *pages*, whilst **Magellan** refer to them as *screens*.
We shall refer to them all as *pages* from now on.

If a page is only shown for one GPS brand, the page is not usually provided by the other manufacturer.

Main Menu

The **Main Menu** allows you to access GPS features such as waypoints, routes, tracks and setup. It will then allow you to use sub menus to explore additional features such as insert, delete and save information. This information can then be retrieved to create routes, TracBack routes and new waypoints.

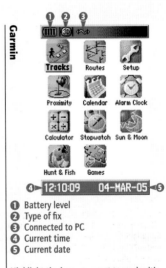

❶ Battery level
❷ Type of fix
❸ Connected to PC
❹ Current time
❺ Current date

Magellan GPS use a menu button to access the main menu. This is shown as a scrollable list.

Highlight the icon you want to work with, press **Enter** and you will go to a dedicated page(s).

Satellite Page

MAIN PAGES

The **Satellite Page** tells you how many satellites the GPS is receiving from and where they are in the sky relative to your position. The following information is shown for each satellite: identifying number, whether the satellite is WAAS, signal strength and whether you have a 2D or 3D fix.

Garmin

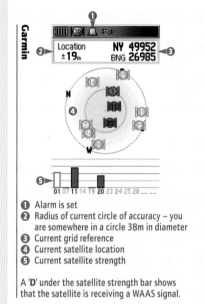

❶ Alarm is set
❷ Radius of current circle of accuracy – you are somewhere in a circle 38m in diameter
❸ Current grid reference
❹ Current satellite location
❺ Current satellite strength

A '**D**' under the satellite strength bar shows that the satellite is receiving a WAAS signal.

Magellan

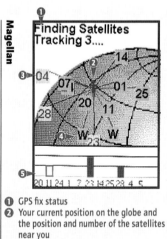

❶ GPS fix status
❷ Your current position on the globe and the position and number of the satellites near you
❸ Satellites being tracked
❹ W on satellites shows they are WAAS (EGNOS)
❺ The strength of signal received from each satellite number

Compass Page

Provided that you are moving at more than about 2km/h and you are navigating towards a waypoint then the compass ring on the **Compass Page** will orientate correctly. It will display the name or number of the waypoint you are navigating towards and the bearing pointer arrow will indicate the direction to the waypoint. Heading information, together with other navigational information, can also be displayed on this screen depending on the model of GPS.

If your GPS has an electronic compass it will give an accurate bearing even when you are stationary provided it is calibrated correctly and is switched on.

In any GPS, the compass ring will orientate correctly when you are moving even if you are not navigating so you can see your direction of travel. You will usually only see a bearing pointer when you are navigating.

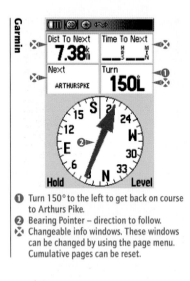

Garmin

❶ Turn 150° to the left to get back on course to Arthurs Pike.
❷ Bearing Pointer – direction to follow.
✗ Changeable info windows. These windows can be changed by using the page menu. Cumulative pages can be reset.

Magellan

❶ Waypoint being navigated to (empty here)
❷ Current position of the sun
❸ Current position of the moon
✗ Changeable info windows. These windows can be changed by using the page menu. Cumulative pages can be reset.

Map Page

MAIN PAGES

When logged onto the satellite system, your current position is marked with a cursor, usually a triangle, on the **Map Page**. This screen can be scrolled or panned (sometimes through a sub-menu) or zoomed in or out. You may need to zoom in quite a lot to see the detail of your route and track in sufficient detail to make sense of it. Look at the map scale in the bottom left hand corner of the screen.

We strongly advise setting this display to **Track Up**. In this mode your route will always be orientated towards the top of the screen on the map/plot screen; in other words, ahead of you. This will give you the best view of your journey ahead. Because your journey may be in any direction a North pointer is shown to help to orientate you.

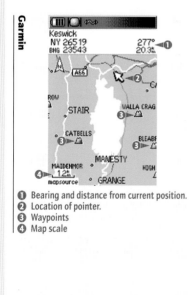

❶ Bearing and distance from current position.
❷ Location of pointer.
❸ Waypoints
❹ Map scale

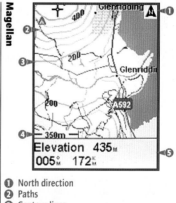

❶ North direction
❷ Paths
❸ Contour lines
❹ Scale of map
❺ Window showing:
  • current altitude: 435m;
  • bearing to next waypoint: 005° magnetic;
  • distance to next waypoint: 172km.

Trip Computer Page

The **Trip Computer Page** records a
variety of navigational data that can
be shown in windows on various pages
according to the GPS model. Some GPS
have a special page for this. The choice
of data and number of data windows to
be shown can be personalised depending
on the GPS model. This data should
normally be reset so that any
information you see relates to the
current journey only.

Magellan GPS Position Page provides
similar information, *see opposite*.

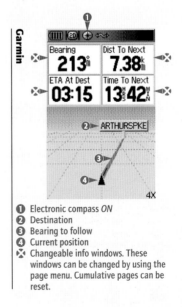

★ All these windows can be changed by
using the page menu. Cumulative pages
can be reset.

Highway Page

The **Highway Page** shows the route
ahead as though it was on a road taking
you point by point to your final
destination. As you progress forward
towards each waypoint on your route,
the road diagram will show the direction
in which you should turn to stay on
course. You can zoom in and out using
a five scale setting to get the detail
you want.

The page also includes up to four user-
selectable data fields, so that you can
see the information that is most useful
to you.

❶ Electronic compass *ON*
❷ Destination
❸ Bearing to follow
❹ Current position
★ Changeable info windows. These
windows can be changed by using the
page menu. Cumulative pages can be
reset.

Barometer/Altimeter Page

MAIN PAGES

If you have a Garmin GPS with sensors, you will be able to see either an altitude view or a barometric pressure view on the **Barometer/Altimeter Page**. On the altitude page, you can view a trend graph showing the altitude profile over time. You can see the total ascent, maximum elevation and current barometric pressure adjusted for altitude. If you switch to the barometer page, you are presented with a trend graph showing the barometric pressure profile over time (up to 48 hours on some models). This can be very useful for forecasting weather changes.

Position Page

The **Position Page** gives you a key snapshot based on your current position – grid reference, elevation, GPS accuracy, date and time, trip odometer and battery status.

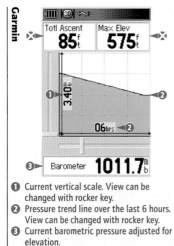

❶ Current vertical scale. View can be changed with rocker key.
❷ Pressure trend line over the last 6 hours. View can be changed with rocker key.
❸ Current barometric pressure adjusted for elevation.
✖ Changeable info windows. These windows can be changed by using the page menu. Cumulative pages can be reset.

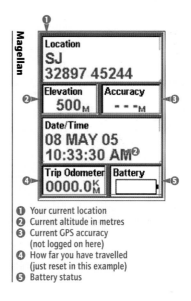

❶ Your current location
❷ Current altitude in metres
❸ Current GPS accuracy (not logged on here)
❹ How far you have travelled (just reset in this example)
❺ Battery status

Setting up your GPS

The Setup function is usually accessed from the main menu. Each GPS model may have a slightly different method of setup.

In general terms, every GPS needs the following setup information:
- the continent or country where you are;
- the coordination, position format or grid system together with the map datum to be used;
- the time zone you are in;
- the navigation units being used;
- the North reference you wish to use.

There will be other personal choices to make on how you prefer your displays, but the above is the critical information required for a GPS to function correctly. We recommend using *Metric* as your display unit as OS maps use metric with *Magnetic* as your North Reference so that you can check the bearing that your GPS gives you with your compass if necessary. If your GPS should suddenly stop working, you can set your compass to the same bearing as you were navigating with your GPS (you will need to remember this) and carry on.

Setting other displays

Having set up the critical features of your GPS properly, you can now make some decisions on how the information created by your GPS is to be displayed. These choices will cover issues such as: the size of the compass on the screen; choosing between an am/pm or 24-hour clock; whether you prefer miles/knots/km; if you like the audible alarm on or off and the setting to be used; setting the displays on your trip computer and the size of text on various screens.

The best approach is to deal with the critical settings and leave the others until later when you have had time to digest all the options that are available to you.

expert tip

The correct setup information for the UK is:
Position Format: **British Grid**
Map Datum: **OSGB**
Time Zone: **London**

expert tip

If you use your GPS abroad it will need to be re-setup to work properly in the new location. Don't forget to reset it when you get home!

expert tip

Personalise your GPS
Some GPS will give you the option of entering 'owner information'. If you do this, your GPS will display your personal details (do include a contact phone number) every time you switch on. Should you ever lose your GPS you'll be glad you did this. You can find out how to do this on the following pages:

Garmin GPS – page 49
Magellan GPS – page 53

SETTING UP YOUR GPS ▼

⚡GARMIN.

Setup Procedure 1* Map Settings, Distance/Speed & Time

1

Choose **Setup** from the main menu. Highlight **Units ❶** and press **Enter**.

2

Position Format
British Grid ❷ ▾
Map Datum
Ord Srvy GB ❸
Distance/Speed
Metric ▾
Elevation (Vert. Speed)
Meters (m/min) ▾
Depth
Feet ▾
Temperature
Fahrenheit ▾
Pressure
Millibars ▾

If you are using your GPS in the UK, highlight **Position Format ❷** & select *British Grid* from the list & press **Enter**.

Many GPS will now automatically change the map datum setting to *Ord. Srvy GB*. If yours does not do this, highlight **Map Datum ❸** and change this. Now press **Enter** to confirm.

3

Position Format
British Grid ▾
Map Datum
Ord Srvy GB
Distance/Speed
Metric ❹ ▾
Elevation (Vert. Speed)
Meters (m/min) ❺ ▾
Depth
Feet ▾
Temperature
Fahrenheit ▾
Pressure
Millibars ▾

You may wish to change the other settings on this page. It is recommended that you use the *Metric* setting for **Distance/Speed ❹** and for **Elevation ❺** as OS maps use these measures.

4

Now choose **Time** from the **Setup** menu. Highlight **Time Zone ❻** and select *London*. You may wish to change the the **Time Format ❼** to suit your preferences.

* These **Setup Procedures** diagrams show our suggested main settings. There are several other setup features that can be used to tailor your GPS to your needs.

Setup Procedure 2 *
Bearing & Heading

&GARMIN.

1

Choose **Heading ❶** from the **Setup** menu and press **Enter**.

2

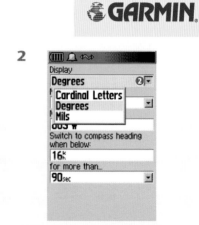

Highlight **Display ❷** & press **Enter**. We suggest that you choose *Degrees* to get a more accurate bearing. If you think that N, NW, SE and so on will be sufficient, then choose *Cardinal Letters*.

3

Highlight **North Reference ❸** & press **Enter**. We suggest that you choose *User* to take magnetic variation into account. Now press **Enter** to set the magnetic variation.

4

Enter the correct magnetic variation (at 2005 = approx 4° West) by choosing the numbers from the grid ❹.
Use the up/down arrows ❺ to select **W** or **E**. Highlight **OK ❻** and press **Enter** to complete the operation. Don't forget to take this variation into account when creating a bearing using your compass.

* These **Setup Procedures** diagrams show our suggested main settings. There are several other setup features that can be used to tailor your GPS to your needs.

&GARMIN.

*Setup Procedure 3
Map Screen

1

Choose **Map ❶** from the **Set Up** menu.
Highlight **Map** and press **Enter**.

2

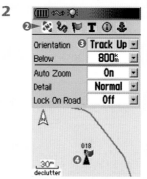

Move the cursor to the first symbol at the top of
the screen ❷ & press **Enter**. Now highlight the
Orientation window and press **Enter**. Select
Track Up ❸ so that your track & route will
always be shown running from bottom to top of
the screen with your position cursor ❹ always
pointing in front of you.

3

Move the cursor to the second symbol at the top
of the screen ❺ & press **Enter**. Now highlight
the **Go To Line** window and press **Enter**. Select
Bearing ❻ so that your route line will be
projected on the basis of the bearing to the next
waypoint.

4

Move the cursor to the fourth symbol at the top
of the screen ❼ & press **Enter**. Now highlight
the **User Waypoints** window and press **Enter**.
Select *Small* ❽ so that you will be able to see
the labels of your waypoints without them being
so big that they will block other information on
the screen.

Setup Procedure 4* (Depending on GPS model)
Calibrating the Electronic Compass

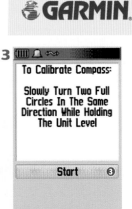

1

Choose **Setup** from the main menu, then choose **Calibration** ❶ and press **Enter**.

2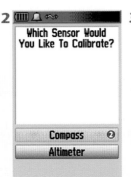

Which Sensor Would You Like To Calibrate?

Compass ❷
Altimeter

Highlight the sensor you wish to calibrate ❷ and press **Enter**.

3

To Calibrate Compass:

Slowly Turn Two Full Circles In The Same Direction While Holding The Unit Level

Start ❸

Highlight **Start** ❸ and press **Enter**. Follow the on-screen instructions. It is not necessary to have a position fix to calibrate the compass. You may just turn the compass around in the palm of your hand to undertake the calibrate process.

4

Turn Slowly... ❹

Just Right
❺

Look at the screen during the process and react to the instructions given ❹ & ❺. If the GPS is being turned too fast or too slow you will be told.

5

Calibration Completed Successfully

OK ❻

The GPS will inform you when the process has been completed successfully. Highlight **OK** ❻ and press **Enter** to finish the procedure.

NOTE: The electronic compass will need re-calibrating at regular intervals and every time you change the batteries, so check it periodically against your compass. Do not hold or store your compass near your GPS as a false reading will be given and, over time, the accuracy of both instruments may be affected.

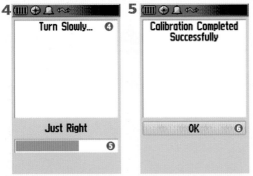

* These **Setup Procedures** diagrams show our suggested main settings. There are several other setup features that can be used to tailor your GPS to your needs.

SETTING UP YOUR GPS

GARMIN.

Setup Procedure 5* (Depending on GPS model)
Calibrating the Barometric Altimeter

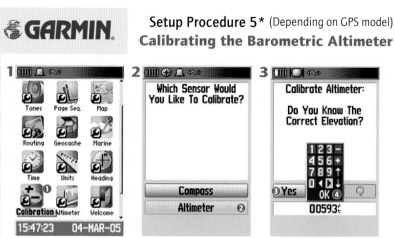

1 Choose **Setup** from the main menu, then choose **Calibration** ❶ and press **Enter**.

2 Which Sensor Would You Like To Calibrate?

Compass

Altimeter ❷

Highlight the sensor you wish to calibrate ❷ and press **Enter**.

3 Calibrate Altimeter:

Do You Know The Correct Elevation?

❸Yes   OK❹

00593

If you know your current elevation, respond **Yes** ❸ and enter it via the grid. Click on **OK** ❹ when finished.

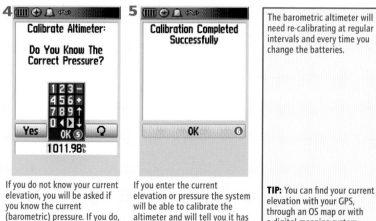

4 Calibrate Altimeter:

Do You Know The Correct Pressure?

Yes   OK❺

1011.98

If you do not know your current elevation, you will be asked if you know the current (barometric) pressure. If you do, enter it via the grid. Click on **OK** ❺ when finished.

5 Calibration Completed Successfully

OK   ❻

If you enter the current elevation or pressure the system will be able to calibrate the altimeter and will tell you it has done so. Highlight the **OK** line and press **Enter** ❻ to finish the process.

The barometric altimeter will need re-calibrating at regular intervals and every time you change the batteries.

TIP: You can find your current elevation with your GPS, through an OS map or with a digital mapping system.

Changing the View in an Information Window

&GARMIN.

1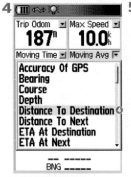

Press and release the **Page** button several times until you see the **Trip Computer** page on the screen. The GPS view here is the *Small Numbers* option.

2

To show just three large information windows, press the **Menu** button & select *Big Numbers* ❶. To change the content of any or all of the information windows, highlight *Change Data Fields* ❷ and press the **Enter** button.

3

You will see that there is a drop down arrow in the top right hand corner of each info. window ❸. Highlight the window you wish to change and press the **Enter** button.

4

Scroll down the list of information that could be shown in the window until you find what you want to be displayed ❹. Press the **Enter** button to complete the process.

5

You can now see that the type of information being shown in the window you were were working on has now changed ❺.

Any information that is cumulative is updated even though it may not be displayed. You can always reveal it after an outing to gather important data about your trip.

* These **Setup Procedures** diagrams show our suggested main settings. There are several other setup features that can be used to tailor your GPS to your needs.

Personalising your GPS

1

From the Main Menu, select **Setup ❶**.

2

With the **Setup** menu on the screen scroll down & highlight the **Welcome Message** icon ❷ and press the **Enter** button.

3

Use the grid to enter the welcome message you wish to appear. The system centres the text automatically when the process is completed. When done, highlight **OK ❸** and press the **Enter** button.

4

GPSmap 60CS
④ SIMON BROWN
GPS TRAINING - UK

TEL 01768 867687

REWARD IF FOUND-
WWW.GPSTRAINING
.CO.UK

Recreational Routable Highway
Basemap, Atlantic v2 2.00
@AND DATA IRELAND, LTD. 2003
@1993-2001, NAVIGATION
TECHNOLOGIES B.V. ALL RIGHTS
RESERVED.

The welcome message will appear on the screen every time your GPS is switched on ❹. The message can be edited or removed at any time by repeating this process.

Setup Procedure 1* Map Settings, Distance/Speed & Time

◄MAGELLAN►

1

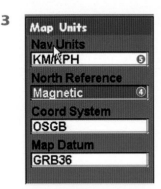

Preferences
Restart GPS
Active Setup
Map Units ①
Pwr Management
Personalize
Language
Clear Memory
Alarms & Beeper
Clock

Press the **Menu** button. Select **Preferences** then **Map Units** ①.

2

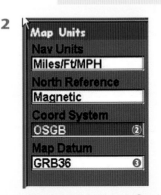

Map Units
Nav Units
Miles/Ft/MPH
North Reference
Magnetic
Coord System
OSGB ②
Map Datum
GRB36 ③

Highlight the **Coord System** window ② and press **Enter**. Select *OSGB* and *1 Metre* if you want a 10 digit grid reference. The **Map Datum** ③ will change automatically to the correct setting *GRB36*.

3

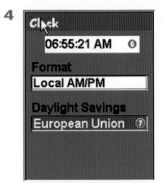

Map Units
Nav Units
KM/KPH ⑤
North Reference
Magnetic ④
Coord System
OSGB
Map Datum
GRB36

Now highlight the **North Ref** window ④ and press **Enter**. Select *Magnetic*.
Next, highlight the **Nav Units** window ⑤ and press **Enter**. We suggest that you choose *KM/KPH* so that you GPS will work best with your OS map.

4

Clock
06:55:21 AM ⑥
Format
Local AM/PM
Daylight Savings
European Union ⑦

Go back to the **Preferences** menu by pressing the **Esc** button. Select **Clock**. ⑥ Enter the correct time and the format that best suits you e.g *Local 24 Hrs*. Now go to the **Daylight Savings** window ⑦ and select *European Union*.

---

* These **Setup Procedures** diagrams show our suggested main settings. There are several other setup features that can be used to tailor your GPS to your needs.

MAGELLAN®

*Setup Procedure 2
Map Screen Setup

1

Press the **Menu** button, then select **Map Setup** ❶.

2

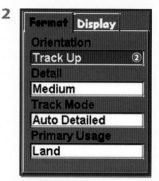

Place your cursor over the **Orientation** window and press the **Enter** button. Select *Track Up* ❷ so that your track & route will always be shown running from bottom to top of the screen with your position cursor always pointing in front of you.

We suggest that you change the other settings as shown above unless you have good reason to change them.

3

Highlight the **Display** tab ❸ to show a list of all the information types that can be shown on the map screen. You may tick or untick each type ❹ to tailor the information you see on your map screen.

Information Windows: Changing Views

1

There are two information windows on both the map and compass screens and all four can be changed to show the information you want to see.

With either of these screens at view, press the **Menu** button, highlight *Customise Page* ❶ and press the **Enter** button.

2

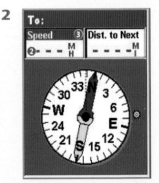

Move the cursor to the information window that you wish to change ❷. You will see the window heading turn blue ❸. Now press the **Enter** button.

3

This step only applies to the windows on the Map Screen.

When you try to change an information window on the map screen, you will be asked how you wish to customise the page. Highlight *customise Fields* ❹ and press the **Enter** button.

4

Scroll up/down the list of information options to highlight the information that you wish to see ❺ and press the **Enter** button.

Repeat the process for any other information window that you wish to change.

Remember that, all data is being computed whether shown or not. You can view data at any time during or immediately after a journey.

MAGELLAN®

Personalising your GPS

1

Press the **Menu** button. Select **Preferences**. Now select **Personalize ❶** to be taken to the next screen.

2

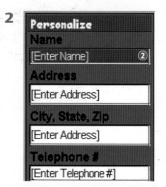

Highlight the first line of the personal details ❷ and press **Enter** to show the data entry screen.

3

Enter your name by highlighting each letter and pressing **Enter**. Note the **Shift**, **Space** and **Back** buttons. ❸ When you have finished, press **OK** ❹ to go back to the **Personalise** screen.

4

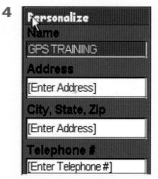

Move the cursor down to the next line of the personal details and enter the data by repeating the last stages. When all the personal data has been entered, press the **Quit** button on your GPS to get back to the menu. The name and tel no will now be shown in the *About* section of the menu. See also *Checking the Software Version* on page 133.

Navigational Data

In most cases a GPS will come with a database holding factory input data as well as space for user-created data. How much information can be stored under each of these headings is governed by the memory capacity of the GPS.

Factory Input Data

All but the basic GPS will have some sort of waypoint database which is built in at the factory. This might be just a list of worldwide 'cities' and their co-ordinates or, in the more up-market models, may include other types such as motorway junctions and so on. 'Cities' is a very general term and could include everything from a small village to a major city. Again this will be dependent on memory size and the basemap installed with the firmware.

Mapping GPS will have more memory and a basemap (usually covering Europe if you buy your GPS there) that is built into the firmware. This cannot usually be updated. In addition there will be the option to import data such as auto navigation, or topo mapping, and additional travel information locations.

User-Created Data

Data created by a user can be grouped into planned data and actual data.

Planned Data – Waypoints/Landmarks and Points of Interest (POI)

The basic GPS navigation unit is a waypoint, landmark or point of interest (POI) and all routes are constructed from these. We will refer to these as waypoints from now on. Each waypoint is held in the GPS database as a unique record of a location that cannot be duplicated with the same name. However one waypoint can be used in many routes. If a waypoint is deleted it will be deleted from any routes containing it. If a route is deleted it does not delete the waypoint in the database as this may be used in another route elsewhere. The number of waypoints and routes that can be stored in a GPS is limited by the model. Typically 500 waypoints and 20 routes can be stored.

Actual Data – Track History/Logs and Saved Tracks

As you progress on your journey, your GPS saves your position data every 30 seconds or so. This data builds up into a track log or track history that is stored in a separate memory area. Chunks of this can be saved as a track and then navigated as a BackTrack or TracBack route. Unwanted track history should be deleted regularly to prevent this database from becoming clogged up. It is good practise to clear your track log before every journey.

Find Page

Highlight the type of waypoint you wish to find and be presented with a list. When in the **Waypoints** page, press **Menu** to select the type of listing you need.

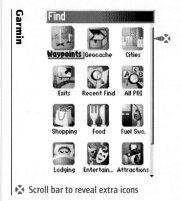

Garmin

❖ Scroll bar to reveal extra icons

How to find saved data

Although this depends on the specific GPS model, the basic principle is to choose the data type you are looking for from the screen menu and, if the command you are looking for is not shown as a button on the screen, then press the menu button to get a list of options about that data type. For instance, choose any waypoint and use the sub-menu to choose from the list of options available such as: edit, add to route, and delete. It's by exploring sub-menus that you find all the little extras a GPS can do.

CHECK YOUR LEARNING

1. Which grid system do we use in the UK?
   a) latitude/longitude
   b) OSGB
   c) WGS 84

2. Which north do we recommend you use?
   a) True
   b) Grid
   c) Magnetic

3. In the UK which time zone do we use?
   a) London
   b) Madrid
   c) New York

4. The map screen should normally be set to:
   a) course up
   b) north up
   c) track up

The answers can be found on page 165.

T A S K :

With your GPS in your hand:
- go into the setup menu and choose 'System';
- reset your GPS to default (usually this is done by choosing 'default' from the menu);
- set up your GPS for use in the UK:
  - is your Position Format set to British Grid or OSGB?
  - is your Time set to London (Garmin only)?
  - set your distance and elevation to metres.

T A S K :

Go outside, power up your GPS and try the following:

Satellite Page
- How many satellites are you locked onto and what are their numbers?
- Have you a 3D fix, or are you 'Ready to Navigate'?

Compass Page
- What other information is displayed on this page?
- Is the compass showing the North position correctly?
- Start walking and see the compass orientate to show the cardinal points correctly

Map Page
- What scale is the map set at?
- Practise zooming in and out
- Can you identify your position on the screen?

Map/Plot Screen settings
- Find the Map/Plot Screen
- Customise screen by setting to Track Up
- Has the orientation of your map changed to scroll ahead of you?
- What scale is your screen showing? (Bottom left)

Trip Computer Page (Garmin) or scroll through the Navigation Pages (Magellan)
- Take a short walk and see what information is displayed:
- How far did you travel?
- How fast were you moving?

View information window
- Find the Information window
- Customise at least two data screens
- Set to Big Numbers if you have this choice
- Restore defaults

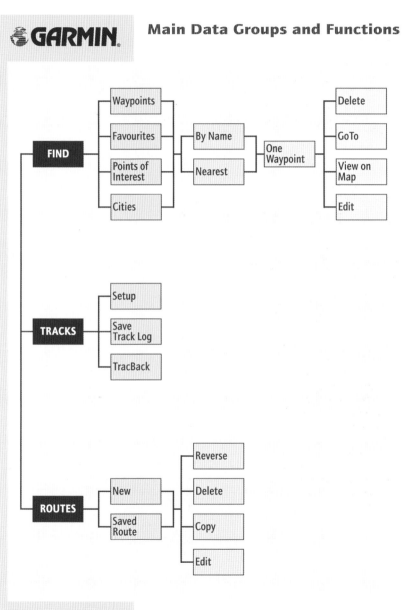

Main Data Groups and Functions

Main Data Groups and Functions

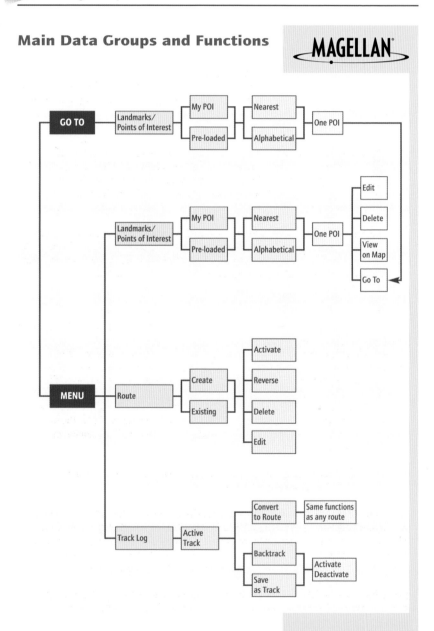

GPS Features and Functions

This is where it starts to get more interesting and hands on. Firstly we will explain the terminology then we will explore what each feature or function actually does and how to optimise its use. There are step-by-step guides on pages 69 to 95 that use diagrams based on copies of real GPS screens to help you to relate theory to practise. Finally there are some practical tasks to complete.

It can be confusing when different manufacturers use different terminology to describe the same thing. A typical example is the waypoint which can be referred to as a mark, landmark, point of interest (POI) or waypoint. Confused? Don't be! Just think of them all as waypoints. In a similar way we will refer to other features and functions by their most commonly used name.

Time spent practising with the GPS in good weather, close to home and in familiar surroundings will help it to become second nature to you, so that you will be up to the task when you need to use it to get you safely back to base in bad conditions. The only way to become familiar with inputting data and using GPS features is practise, practise, and practise.

The **Mark** function   **G: PAGE 70 M: PAGE 84**
This function has two main uses:
- to mark your current position so that it can be stored in your GPS waypoint database. This could be a special location you would like to return to or could be the location of an accident so that the grid reference could be passed on to the rescue services.
- to mark your current position and then change the co-ordinates to create a new location that can then be stored in your GPS waypoint database. This is the only way to get waypoint data into your GPS unless you have a digital mapping or waypoint management system.

As a waypoint, a mark can be navigated to at a later date either as one isolated destination (a **GoTo**) or as a part of a route.

The waypoint is automatically given a consecutive number by the GPS – for example *WPT001*, *WPT002* for **Garmins** or *LMK001*, *LMK002* for some **Magellans**. As these labels can be confusing, rename them to make them easier to be found. GPS names are usually limited to 6–10 characters so it's a good idea to carry a cheap and small A–Z address book to store a more detailed description of important waypoints.

Take a little time to let the GPS 'settle' to get the most accurate reading before you 'mark' it. Some GPS have an 'averaging function' that does this automatically.

Landmarks/Waypoints/Points of Interest (POI)

To keep things simple, we will refer to all of these as waypoints from now on. A waypoint is a mark that might have had user information added to it and is then saved to the user database in the GPS. A waypoint can have the following information:

- Name (6–10 characters dependent on type)
- A symbol/icon. Choose one from the list in your GPS.
- Elevation data
- A grid reference of your choice
- A brief message to be stored. Some models only.

If you use the British Grid System then your position will be expressed as a ten figure OS grid reference, for example NY34214 76408. If you wish you can insert zeros at the end of say a 6 figure grid reference and then save it. For example NY39400 48600. On many GPS, the letters *BNG*, the abbreviation for British National Grid, will be shown by the grid reference.

To create a waypoint for a specific location, just use the **Mark** function and then edit the features, especially the grid reference, to create the waypoint location you want to save. Unless you are storing a mark of your current position as a waypoint, you can create them anywhere, for example, in the comfort of your own home. Creating waypoints on the move isn't easy, especially in poor weather conditions, so practise indoors whilst you can.

WAYPOINT LEARNING TASK 1

a) Go outdoors and create a waypoint of your current location using the **Mark** function.
- What is your current grid reference?
- What is the number of this waypoint on the screen? Remember it before you save it.
- What elevation are you at?

b) Save the waypoint to your GPS database.

Waypoints

You can work with way-points as follows:

- name and save a waypoint to the user database;
- edit waypoint data;
- find a waypoint in the user database;
- delete a waypoint;
- navigate (**GoTo**) to any waypoint in your user database;
- add waypoints together to form a route;
- view waypoints on the Map or Plot screen;
- see how far away a waypoint is from your current position and the bearing to it.

Details of where to find diagrams illustrating these functions on each system can be found on page 68.

e x p e r t   t i p

Remember a GPS will happily navigate straight over a cliff!
It has no idea what hazards are between A and B so you will have to think for it. Refer to your map and either contour round or follow the logical line or nearest footpath to your destination.

Waypoint Learning Task 1 continued

c) Having created a waypoint and saved it into your database, you must be able to find it again. For Garmin look in **FIND** then *Nearest* or *By Name*. For Magellan look in **MENU** then *Landmarks* then *User*.

With the waypoint record on the screen, you can:
- access its navigation information;
- navigate to it with the **GoTo** function;
- edit the information if required.

WAYPOINT LEARNING TASK 2

a) Whilst indoors create four or five waypoints based on features in your locality that can later be linked together as a route that you could walk in say half an hour. Follow the instructions in the next paragraph to do this. You can do this by creating a mark for each one that you then edit and save to your GPS database. Do not make the first and last waypoints the same location. Look at the detailed instructions below before you start. You will be navigating this route later so choose waypoints, such as church, pub and so on, with care.

Get the grid reference for each of the four/five locations from your paper map and transfer the data into the grid below so that you have the data to refer to as you key it into your GPS. Remember you will need both the grid letters and numbers for each. You will probably not be able to work out a 10 digit grid reference so simply put zeros after each set to make it up to ten digits, for example NY 40630 38670. Remember you probably have a maximum of 6–10 characters for the name dependant on which GPS you have. Choose a name and symbol/icon for each waypoint based on the list you have in your GPS.

Waypoint Name	Symbol/Icon	Grid Reference	
		Letters	Numbers

b) Find the saved mark from Task 1 on page 60 and delete it. Do not delete the waypoints saved earlier in this Task 2 as we will be working with them later.

The **GoTo** Function   G: PAGE **72** M: PAGE **87**

This is one of the most important functions of the GPS as it gets the GPS to navigate you to a waypoint. It is simple to activate but complex in the information it can give you. Here you will start to see what the GPS can do. The more you get to grips with this feature, the more uses you will find for it. Once you have a 3D satellite fix, find any waypoint from your user database and then select the **GoTo** function. Once you are moving (unless your GPS has an electronic compass), your GPS will now:

- give you a direct line bearing or direction arrow (on the compass page) to your destination. This bearing will be dynamic as it updated every second. This means it is self-correcting according to your current location;
- countdown the current distance to the destination;
- show your current position and the destination position on the plot or map screen. You will also see the breadcrumb trail (your track so far).

G O T O   T A S K

a) Go outdoors and find one of the waypoints you have created.

b) Activate the **GoTo** function to navigate towards it.

c) Show the Compass Page on the screen. What information do you see on this screen?

d) Walk in the direction of the compass pointer. How is the information changing as you walk?

e) Scroll to the Map Page and zoom in/out until you can see both your current position and your destination. What is the scale on the map at this point?

Making the best use of the GoTo function:

- Find the approximate location on your paper map of the waypoint you have told your GPS to GoTo.
- Look at the ground between your present position and your destination.
- Make life easy for yourself and contour around obstacles.
- As you contour, your GPS will update your direction pointer.
- When you think you have arrived, allow your GPS time to settle and your estimated position error will improve. This will make your position information more accurate.
- Try to get out of the shadow of trees or buildings if you can to ensure the clearest view of the sky.

Details of where to find diagrams illustrating these functions on each system can be found on page 68.

The **Route** function allows you to:

- create a route;
- edit a route – insert and delete waypoints ;
- alter the position of a waypoint in the route;
- view the route on the map screen;
- navigate a route;
- calculate the area of a circular route (on some models);
- reverse a route;
- delete the whole route.

Details of where to find diagrams illustrating these functions on each system can be found on page 68.

The **Route** Function   G: PAGE 73 M: PAGE 88

A route is a number of waypoints linked together in a predetermined order. The straight-line section of the route between any two waypoints is called a leg. An average GPS will allow you to save up to 20 routes.

Route creation is a relatively simple process as the GPS does most of the work. All you have to do is feed waypoints into the new route in the order you wish to follow them. A GPS will allow you to insert waypoints directly from your user database into an empty route screen.

When your GPS is navigating in **Route** mode it is basically doing a series of **GoTos**. It will recognise the next waypoint in the route automatically and navigate from one waypoint to the next. It will also show you on the map screen that you are closer to **Waypoint 2** than to **3** for instance – a useful indication of your position within the route. However, the point at which your GPS 'clicks' onto the next waypoint in the route can seem a little random.

The reason for this is that the GPS has an ever-varying 'circle of accuracy' and could start navigating you to the next waypoint at any point within that circle. This could either be before or after the actual location of the previous waypoint. In general terms, when the accuracy of the GPS is very high the circle of accuracy will be correspondingly very small. The result should be that the GPS will start navigating to the next waypoint much nearer to the actual position of the preceding waypoint. This principle should be borne in mind when route planning.

A route can be created in one of two ways, either manually or through a Digital Mapping System/Waypoint Management System downloaded via a cable into your GPS in seconds. We will explore this option in depth in *Chapter 5, Digital maps explained* on page 97.

R O U T E   T A S K

a) Create a route using the waypoints created in Task 2 then save the route.
   (The route is saved automatically only on the Garmin GPS.)

b) Go outside and activate or start navigation of the route you have created.

c) Find the Compass Page. What is the distance and bearing to your next waypoint?

d) Note the points at which your GPS 'clicks' over automatically to navigate you to the next waypoint in your route. How accurate is the GPS in navigating you to each waypoint and to your destination?

e) When you are at your destination, reverse the route. Look at the detail of the route and check that the waypoints are now listed in reverse order?

f) Activate/Navigate the reversed route to get back to your original starting point.

g) As you are walking, zoom in on the map screen so that you can see your position and the rest of your route ahead of you.

h) When you return to base, deactivate or stop navigating the route you have just walked.

i) Delete the route

j) Find one of the waypoints used in the route to prove that even though the route has been deleted the waypoints are still there.

The **Track** Function   **G: PAGE 79 M: PAGE 94**

Whilst your GPS is receiving a 3D fix, its position is being updated every second. This information is also being recorded every 30 seconds as a track history or track log of where you have been. This can be viewed on the **Map** screen in real time as a bread-crumb trail. The correct term for this with **Magellan GPS** is a track or track route.

The track history comes alive if you have a digital mapping system and a PC. While on your walk keep your GPS switched on with a 3D fix. After the walk, save your track to your PC, convert it into a route, print out the section of the OS map with your route on it and then, if you wish, share it with your friends by e-mail. You can return to the route at any time in the future by saving it into a folder of your favourite routes on your PC.

What if you could review your day's walk, compare it with your paper map and digital map, tell what speed you were travelling at and what time you were at any place in your log? All this is possible with the **track** function if you have a digital mapping system such as ***Memory-Map***. *Chapter 5, Digital maps explained* on page 97 looks at digital mapping systems in more detail.

e x p e r t   t i p

The **BackTrack** or **TracBack** can be navigated as a route taking you back virtually over the ground you walked on whereas a reversed route may not keep you on the actual path you trod on the way out.

e x p e r t   t i p

Spend some time getting used to the track function. It is very powerful and will prove very helpful to you even if you don't have a digital mapping system. Remember to clear your track history/log at the start of each day.

e x p e r t   t i p

A quick way of getting back to base, without having to remember which buttons to press, is to navigate back by following your breadcrumb trail line backwards by looking at the Map/Plot screen. Zoom in so that you can see immediately if you wander off the track line.

The track history/log function allows you to:

- record your movement across the ground as a track history or track log;
- display the log as a breadcrumb trail (dotted line) in the map or plot view;
- when the track memory is full, the oldest part of the track is deleted to make space for inserting the newest track. This can be set up in different ways;
- save all or part of your track history/log as a track route or track;
- clear the log whenever you like. Saved tracks will not be affected;
- delete any or all of the saved track;
- reverse a saved track so it can be navigated in reverse (to get back to base, for example). This is called a *TracBack* (Garmin) or *BackTrack* (Magellan);
- download the log into a digital mapping system so that you can review your performance (position, elevation, time and date, speed);
- with *Memory-Map*, you can convert a track to a route on the PC screen.

T R A C K S   T A S K   1

a) Show the tracks page on your GPS screen.
b) Save all of your track (this may include many walks if you haven't cleared it recently).
c) Now clear your Track Log (Track with Magellan).
d) Go on a short walk and observe your new track log as it builds up on the map/plot screen as you are on the move.
e) On your return save your track.

T R A C K S   T A S K   2

a) Clear your Track Log (Track with Magellan)

b) Go on a short walk and stop at the point before you turn back towards home

c) Activate a TracBack or backtrack route based on your track log/track

d) Navigate using this to get you back to base. Observe your TracBack/backtrack on the Map/Plot Screen whilst on the move. How closely is the GPS navigating you back?

e) When you are back home, stop navigation or deactivate your route.

If you saved your track, delete it from your GPS.

04

Step-by-Step User Guide

These pictorial step-by-step guides,
which use actual screen shots
from **Garmin** and **Magellan** GPS,
should help you develop your
practical GPS skills and be
a useful source of reference
in the future.

Introduction

We have developed these unique step-by-step guides with you, the user, in mind. They explain in sequence how you can get the GPS to do something correctly. By using special 'screen grab' images you can see exactly what the screen of the GPS should look like as you progress through each function. We start with the very basic tasks and move forward in a logical way to more advanced GPS features.

Above: *Garmin eTrex Legend C and Vista C GPS receivers.*

The 'screen grabs' are based on the **Garmin eTrex Legend C** and **Vista C** ranges. The **Magellan** diagrams are based on the **eXplorist 500** and **600** GPS. No matter what GPS you own, you should find that the screens are similar to yours so these step-by-steps should be useful to all.

Although this book is not waterproof, it has been designed to fit into a typical rucksack so that you can carry it with you for use outdoors.

Above: *Magellan eXplorist 500 and 600 GPS receivers.*

GARMIN	
Resetting the Trip Computer	**69**
Manually Marking & Entering a Waypoint	**70**
Finding a Waypoint	**71**
GoTo or Delete a Waypoint	**72**
Creating a Route	**73**
Amending a Route	**74**
Navigating a Route	**75**
Stopping Navigation of a Route	**76**
Reversing a Route	**77**
Deleting a Route	**78**
Saving a Track Log to a Saved Track	**79**
Clearing the Track Log Before You Set Off	**80**
Creating & Navigating a TracBack Route	**81**

MAGELLAN	
Magellan GPS File Storage System	**82**
Resetting the Trip Computer	**83**
Manually Marking & Entering a Waypoint (POI*)	**84**
Finding a Waypoint	**85**
Edit or Delete a Waypoint	**86**
Creating a GoTo Route	**87**
Creating a Route	**88**
Amending a Route	**89**
Navigating a Route	**90**
Stopping Navigation of a (GoTo) Route	**91**
Reversing a Route	**92**
Deleting a Route	**93**
Track Log: Clearing the Active Track/ Backtracking on Active Track/ Saving Active Track	**94**
Finding & Navigating a Saved Track	**95**

Resetting the Trip Computer

1

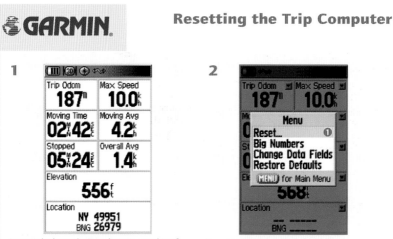

Press and release the **Page** button a number of times until you see the **Trip Computer** page on the screen.

2

Press the **Menu** button to show the trip computer menu. Highlight *Reset* ❶ and then press **Enter**.

3

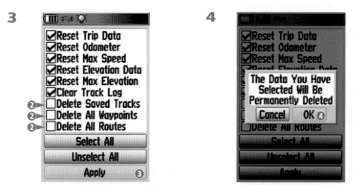

4

When you first reset the trip computer you will need to check the boxes that you want to be reset each time you undertake the reset process. We suggest that you follow the layout of the screen above. You are urged not to check the last three lines ❷ as this data would be very difficult to reinstate if it was deleted by mistake.

As the **Apply** line is already highlighted ❸, just press the **Enter** key to reset.

You will be asked to confirm this operation so highlight **OK** ❹ and press the **Enter** button to complete the process.

Manually Marking & Entering a Waypoint

If the mark is of the current location, just click on **OK ❷** to save it.

Depending on the model of GPS, choose **Mark** at the main menu, or by pressing the click stick or by pressing the **Mark** button. The next waypoint number and its details appear, ready for changing; *see above* – in this example, it is called number *018*. Move the cursor down to the **name/number** position ❶ ready for making a change. Next to it is the waypoint symbol. This can be changed too.

Note the **Back** and **Forward** arrows ❸ to move the cursor.

To change the number to a name – in this example *018* to *PUB* – press **Enter** or press down on the click stick. Select the letters/numbers you need from the grid by using the click stick or the **Up/Down** buttons & the **Enter** key. Then click on **OK ❹** to end this part of the editing.

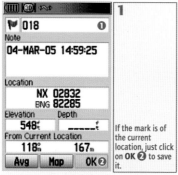

Next, the grid reference ❺ can be changed. First the letters, if necessary, use the *Up/Down* arrows ❻ then the numbers. Again click on **OK** to end this part of the editing.
Note that *BNG*=British National Grid

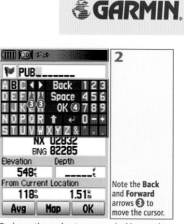

Other parts of the waypoint can be changed, as indicated by the ✖. When you have finished editing the waypoint, press OK ❼ to save the waypoint to the database. It can now be used as a GoTo or as part of a route. The waypoint can always be changed again at any time or deleted.

❽ Waypoint icon

&GARMIN.

Finding a Waypoint

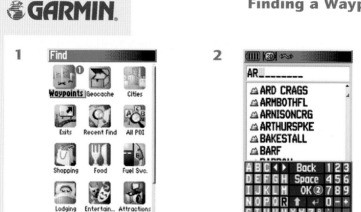

Press the **Find** button to show the **Find** menu. Highlight **Waypoints** ❶ from this menu, then press **Enter**. You will now see a list of waypoints either *By Name* or *Nearest*, decided by your choice the last time you used the menu in Step 2.

The default setting is to show waypoints *by name* in alphabetical order. Place the cursor over the first letter of the waypoint you wish to find and press **Enter** Then enter the next letter and so on. When you see your waypoint in the list, place the cursor over **OK** ❷ and press **Enter** to close the grid. Highlight the desired waypoint and press **Enter** to bring up the details on screen.

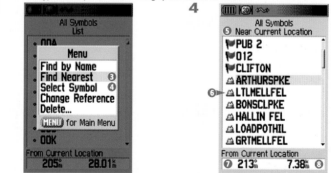

If you wish to see the waypoints listed in another way, press the **Enter** key whilst showing the *by name* listing. Choose how you would like to view the waypoints and press **Enter**.

If you choose *Find Nearest* ❸ you will be shown a list ❺ of the nearest 50 waypoints in the order of how close they are to your current location. As each waypoint is highlighted, you are shown the bearing ❼ and the distance to it ❽.

If you choose *Select Symbol* ❹, you can select the symbol from a list and then get a list of all waypoints using that symbol. For example, just those having a *Summit* symbol ❻.

Highlight the desired waypoint and press **Enter** to bring the details up on to the screen.

GoTo or Delete a Waypoint

GARMIN.

1

Find the waypoint you need by following the step-by-step instructions on the *Finding a Waypoint* diagram on page 71. The steps are summarised below.

2

AR_____

⛰ ARD CRAGS
⛰ ARMBOTHFL
⛰ ARNISONCRG
⛰ ARTHURSPKE
⛰ BAKESTALL
⛰ BARF

A B C ◄ ► Back 1 2 3
D E F G H Space 4 5 6
I J K L M OK ① 7 8 9
N O P Q R ↑ ↵ □ – +
S T U V W X Y Z & ' .

• Press **Find** button
• Highlight **Waypoints**
• Press **Enter** button
• If waypoint is not in list use grid to enter name
• Highlight **OK ①** then press **Enter** button

3

All Symbols
Near Current Location

📍 PUB 2
📍 012
📍 CLIFTON
⛰ ARTHURSPKE ❸
⛰ LTLMELLFEL
⛰ BONSCLPKE
⛰ HALLIN FEL
⛰ LOADPOTHIL
⛰ GRTMELLFEL

From Current Location
213° 7.38ᵏ

• Scroll down list to locate desired waypoint ❷
• Highlight waypoint ❸
• Press **Enter** button to show details of waypoint on GPS screen

4

⛰ ARTHURSPKE

Note

Location
NY 46143
BNG 20656

Elevation   Depth
1748ᶠ   _____ᶠ

From Current Location
213°   7.38ᵏ

Delete   Map   Go To
  ❹   ❺   ❻

When you have selected the desired waypoint, you can:
• See its position on the map ❺
• Navigate to that waypoint location by doing a **GoTo** ❻
• Delete the waypoint from the database ❹

&GARMIN.

Creating a Route ▼

1 Saved Routes

COL TO BOWSC
BANNERDALE BA
BANNERDALE OU
BECKSIDE BACK
BECKSIDE OUT
BLENCATHRA
BROCKHOLE BAC
BROCKHOLE OUT
COPYHILL ROUT
FLAWN – OOA
HART CRAG DOV
NBIELD

New ❶ | Active

From the main menu, select **Routes** and press **Enter**. You will see that the word **New ❶** is already highlighted so just press **Enter** again to select a new route screen.

2

‹Select Next Point›❷

Leg Dist | Leg Time
___k | H___M
     m | R___I
     | S   N

Navigate | **Map**

You will see the *Select Next Point* ❷ already highlighted so press **Enter** again to select the first waypoint to go into the route.

3 ⚑ CLIFTON

Note

Location
NY 53683
BNG 27195
Elevation   Depth
_____ft   _____ft
From Current Location
089°m   3.73k m

Delete | **Map** | **Use ❸**

Follow the instructions on page 71 to find the waypoint you want. With the waypoint details on the screen, press **Use ❸** to insert it into your route.

4 CLIFTN – BNSC   ❹

⚑ CLIFTON
⚑ ARTHURSPKE
⚑ LOADPOTHIL
⚑ BONSCLPKE
‹Select Next Point›

Leg Dist | Leg Time
___k | H___M
     m | R___I
     | S   N

Navigate ❺ | Map

Repeat the previous instructions for each waypoint to go into the route. You will see that the *name* of the route is automatically made up of the first and last waypoint names ❹.

When all waypoints have been entered, you may just press the **Quit** button and the route details will be saved. If you want to follow the route, highlight **Navigate ❺** with the cursor and press **Enter**.

5 CLIFTN – BNSC

A B C ◄ ► Clear 1 2 3
D E F G H Space 4 5 6
I J K L M   OK ❻ 7 8 9
‹Select Next Point›

Leg Dist | Leg Time
0" | H___M
     | R___I
     | S   N

Navigate | Map

To insert a proper name for a route, move the cursor up to the top line and press **Enter**. Pick the characters from the grid by highlighting them and pressing **Enter** until the name has been created. Now highlight **OK ❻** and press **Enter**.

Amending a Route

⊛GARMIN.

1

From the main menu, select **Routes** and press **Enter**. Scroll through your route list ❶ and highlight the route you want to amend. Now press **Enter**.

2

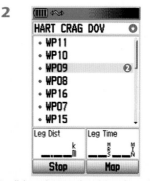

Scroll down the waypoints that make up the route and highlight the one you wish to change in some way ❷ or the place where you wish to insert another waypoint. (The new waypoint will be inserted above the one highlighted). Now press **Enter** to show the amendment menu.

3

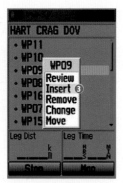

Choose the menu option you need ❸:

- *Review* – Change the details of a waypoint
- *Insert* – Insert a new waypoint above this one
- *Remove* – Delete the waypoint from the route
- *Change* – Replace this waypoint with another
- *Move* – Change the order of this waypoint in the list

When you have completed the amendment(s) needed, just press the **Quit** button to close the screen and the changes are saved automatically.

---

e x p e r t   t i p

To name or rename a route, move the cursor to the *Name* box at the top of the screen *(see* ❶ *in Screen 2 above)* and press **Enter**. Use the grid to create or edit the name and press **Enter** again to finish the process.

⛂ **GARMIN**®

Navigating a Route

1

From the main menu, select **Routes** and press **Enter**. Scroll through your route list and highlight the route you want to navigate ❶. Now press **Enter** to choose this route.

2

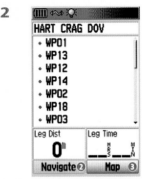

The details of the chosen route are now displayed on the screen. To see the route on the map highlight the **Map** button ❸ and press **Enter**. To navigate the route, highlight **Navigate** ❷ and press **Enter**. This route is now called the 'active' route.

3

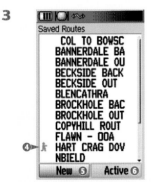

If you wish to see which route is active or change the active route, select **Routes** at the main menu. You will see a figure by the *active route* ❹. To change the active route, highlight **New** ❺ and press enter. Select the new route and press **Enter**. To view the details of the active route, highlight **Active** ❻ and press **Enter**.

4 **NOTE:**
A route will remain active even if the GPS is switched off. It can only be stopped by following these instructions.

See also *Stopping Navigation of a Route* on page 76

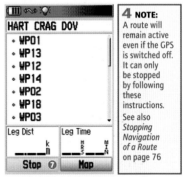

To stop navigating the active route, either:
• press and release the page key until the active route page is shown; or
• follow the instructions to the left.
Now highlight the **Stop** button ❼ and press **Enter**

Stopping Navigation of a Route

There are several ways to stop navigating a route and these are shown below.
NOTE: A route will remain active even if the GPS is switched off and switched back on again.
It can only be stopped by following these instructions.

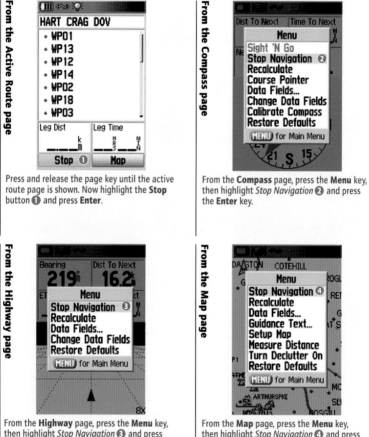

From the Active Route page

Press and release the page key until the active route page is shown. Now highlight the **Stop** button ❶ and press **Enter**.

From the Compass page

From the **Compass** page, press the **Menu** key, then highlight *Stop Navigation* ❷ and press the **Enter** key.

From the Highway page

From the **Highway** page, press the **Menu** key, then highlight *Stop Navigation* ❸ and press the **Enter** key.

From the Map page

From the **Map** page, press the **Menu** key, then highlight *Stop Navigation* ❹ and press the **Enter** key.

GARMIN.

STOPPING NAVIGATING/REVERSING A ROUTE ▼ GARMIN

All routes can be reversed even if they are not active. For example you may wish to walk a route the opposite way round this time. These instructions apply to reversing the active route but the same principles can be applied to any route.

1

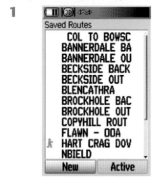

From the main menu, select **Routes** and press **Enter**. Press **Enter** again to show the details of the active route.

2

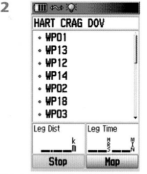

With the details of the active route shown on the screen, press the **Menu** button to show the route menu.

3

Highlight *Reverse Route* ❶ and press the **Enter** button.

4

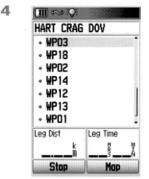

The order of the waypoints making up the routes are now reversed so that it can be navigated back to base from the current position or navigated in reverse.

Deleting a Route

When a route is deleted, the waypoints making it up remain in the database of the GPS.

1

From the main menu, select **Routes** and press **Enter**. Scroll down the list of routes and highlight the route that you want to delete. Press the **Enter** button to show the details of the route.

2

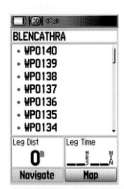

With the details of the selected route shown on the screen, press the **Menu** button to show the route menu.

3

Highlight *Delete Route* ❶ and press the **Enter** button. The route is now deleted from the GPS database.

⚜GARMIN.

Saving a Track Log as a Saved Track

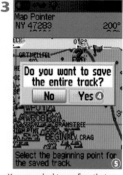

1

Tracks ● Routes Setup
Proximity Calendar Alarm Clock
Calculator Stopwatch Sun & Moon
Hunt & Fish Games
17·08·01   24-MAR-05

At the Main Menu highlight **Tracks ①** and press **Enter**.

2

Track Log   ⦿ On ○ Off
1% ②
Setup | Clear
Save ③ | TracBack
Saved Tracks

20 Unused

The **Track Log** bar **②** shows that 1% of its total memory has been used up since it was last cleared. We will assume that the data held in there represents a record of today's journey. To save this as a separate track file, highlight **Save ③** and press the **Enter** button.

3

Map Pointer
NY 47289   200°
Do you want to save the entire track?
No | Yes ④
Select the beginning point for the saved track. ⑤

You are asked to confirm that you want to save the entire track. You can answer **Yes** to this **④** as you wisely cleared the track log before you set out today. If you had not cleared the track, you would be asked to select the start and end point for the the track to be saved **⑤**.

4

Name
LAKESIDE PATH   ⑥
Distance
8.52ᵏₘ
Area
756.2   ha   ▼
Color
Dk Blue
✓ Show On Map

Delete | Map
TracBack | OK ⑦

Details of the track to be saved are shown. To change the name which shows the date by default, move the cursor up into the name window **⑥** and press **Enter**. You will be able to change the name by using the grid.

5

Track Log   ⦿ On ○ Off
0%
Setup | Clear
Save | TracBack
Saved Tracks
LAKESIDE PATH ⑧

19 Unused ⑨

When finished, highlight **OK ⑦** and press **Enter**. We can now see the saved track with the new name we have given it **⑧**.

The track log builds up a back-to-back record of all your journeys. The record of the track of a journey can be saved as a track file to be used for navigation or analysis later.

We can also see that we have an unused capacity for 19 extra tracks to be saved **⑨** so if we were walking say a long distance footpath, we could save the track each day for up to 20 days.

Clearing the Track Log Before You Set Off

We strongly advise clearing the track log before each outing as it will make working with tracks easier. The track log builds up a back-to-back record of all your journeys. The record of the track of a journey can be saved as a track file to be used for navigation or analysis later. The track log will also be cleared as part of resetting the trip computer *(see page 69)* if the *Clear Track Log* box has been checked.

1

From the main menu, highlight **Tracks ❶** and press the **Enter** button.

2

- The **Track Log** bar ❷ shows how much memory you have currently used.
- There is normally no need to change the default settings.
- To clear/delete the track log, highlight **Clear ❸** and press the **Enter** button.

3

You are asked to confirm that you want to clear the track log, highlight **Yes ❹** and press the **Enter** button.

4

When the track log has been cleared, you will see the memory bar at 0% ❺.

&GARMIN.

1

From the Main Menu select **Tracks**. Now move the cursor on the Tracks screen to highlight the saved track you wish to work with ❶ and press the **Enter** button.

2

You now see the details of the selected track. Move the cursor over **TracBack** ❷ and press the **Enter** button to start to create a TracBack route.

3

You now see the saved track on the screen labelled with the **BEGIN** and **END** positions ❸. Place the cursor over the point you wish to TracBack to (normally the beginning) and press the **Enter** button.

4

The TracBack route is now shown on the screen ❹. You can see that your current position is now labelled as **BEGIN** ❺ as it is the beginning of the TracBack route back to your original starting point.

5

You are now able to use the navigational features of your GPS as normal. Here we show the Highway page which shows the route set out as a 'road' ❻ with each major feature labelled as it approaches your position ❼ shown by the black triangle cursor.

> Waypoints are called **turns** in a TracBack route

Magellan GPS
File Storage System

- Internal Memory
- Secure Digital (SD) Card – installed as extra memory
- Grey if no SD card installed

Background Maps
- Up One Level
- Basemap

Detail Maps
- Up One Level
- Empty

My Points of Interest or Waypoints ⊗
- Up One Level
- New Folder
- New POI Folder
- Default POI Folder

Routes ⊗
- Up One Level
- New Folder
- New Routes Folder
- Default Routes Folder

Track Logs ⊗
- Up One Level
- New Folder
- Active Track

Geocaches ⊗
- Up One Level
- New Folder
- Empty

Magellan uses a computer-like structure for storing data, whether waypoints or points of interest, routes, tracks, geocaches or maps.

- The file system is similar to that used on your computer.

- It is recommended that you store data in the most appropriate folder and that you create new folders to classify data sensibly.

- You may move up and down the folders by highlighting the *Up One Level* line and pressing the **Enter** button.

- Folders marked ⊗ hold their data as ASCII files. When your GPS is connected to a computer it becomes a virtual disk so that data in these files can be edited by using any text editing program.

- To create a new folder, highlight the *new folder* line and press the **Enter** button.

- Folders can be named so you can find data more easily.

- If you have a secure digital (SD) card installed for extra memory, you will have to decide where you store data. Remember, the SD card is removable but the internal memory is not.

- The **DETAIL MAPS** folder can hold sections of detailed topographical map that you may buy as an extra.

- Each map tile or 'cut' can be stored in a separate folder within **DETAIL MAPS**. You may switch between them by selecting the folder you wish to make 'active'.

- You can see which folders are active by choosing *Preferences* then *Active Setup*.

- When your GPS is connected to a computer, you may delete folders or copy them to a computer storage area.

e x p e r t   t i p

Active files can be located immediately. Save yourself time scrolling through the directory by making active the files you use regularly. This is done by selecting *Preferences/Active Setup*, then choosing from a folder the files you wish to change.

MAGELLAN

Resetting the Trip Computer

1

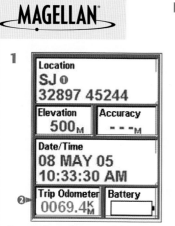

Press the **Screen** button. until the location screen (as above ❶) is seen. The odometer window shows that this user has moved 69.4km ❷ since it was last reset.

2

Press the **Menu** button to show the menu. The *Reset Trip* line is highlighted by default ❸. Press the **Enter** button to reset this.

3

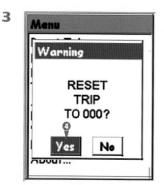

You will be asked to confirm the process. Move the cursor to highlight the **Yes** button ❹ and press the **Enter** button.

4

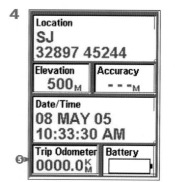

The trip odometer is now reset to zero ❺ ready to log your next outing.

Manually Marking & Entering a Waypoint (POI*)

1

Press the **Mark** button to see your current position. If required, this can be edited before saving. Highlight the window you wish to change ❶ and press **Enter** to see the editing screen.

2

Enter the new data (such as the name) into this screen by placing your cursor over each letter ❷ or number and pressing the **Enter** button. Highlight **OK** ❸ to finish this process and return to the **POI** screen.

3

Now move your cursor down to the next window you wish to change (such as the grid ref.) ❹ and follow the same procedure as in the last stage.

4

Here we can see the three windows that have been changed:
❺ the POI name;
❻ the POI grid reference;
❼ a message about the POI.
We can also change:
• the POI icon   • the POI elevation.
When finished highlight **Save** ❽ and press the **Enter** button.†

---

*POI = Point of Interest.
This is also known as a waypoint or landmark
Your GPS must be logged on to the satellite system to mark your current position successfully. However it does not need to be logged on to just enter the details of POI that you wish to store in your database for later use.

You may find the **Magellan GPS File Storage System** diagram on page 82 helpful.

MARKING & ENTERING/FINDING WAYPOINTS ▼ MAGELLAN

~MAGELLAN~

Finding a Waypoint

1

```
↖Menu
  Pts of Interest        ①
  Routes
  Track Log
  Adv. Features
  Preferences
  Weather
  Help
  About...
```

Press the **Menu** button and highlight *Pts of Interest* ①. Now press the **Enter** button.

2

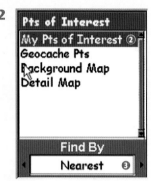

```
Pts of Interest
  My Pts of Interest  ②
  Geocache Pts
  Background Map
  Detail Map

        Find By
     Nearest      ③  ►
```

Highlight *My Pts of Interest* ② and press the **Enter** button. Note that you can search for POIs in two ways ③:
• by Nearest   • by Alphabetic.
You can change the method by highlighting the window at the bottom of the screen and moving the joystick left or right.

3

```
My Pts of Interest
..OIs\Default POI File ◄④
  🗎 Up One Level
  ⊕ POI002          ⑤
  ⊕ POI003
  ⊕ GATE 1
  ⊕ POI005

  Bearing    Distance
   313ᵐ  ⑥   2178ᴷ
```

Your POI will normally be stored in the *Default POI File* ④. This should appear by default. Scroll down the POI list until you are highlighting the one you want ⑤. Note that you are told the bearing and distance from your current location ⑥ (if you are are logged on to the satellite system). Now press the **Enter** key to show the POI details on the screen.

4

```
Edit POI
Vis  Icon  Name
 ✔   ▣  │POI002      │
Location
 SJ
 32896 45244
Elevation
 500ᴹ
Message
 CREATE MESSAGE?

  Save  ⑦    View  ⑧
```

With the detailed POI on the screen you can now edit it as you wish, for example add a message or alter the icon. You may save the POI back to the database ⑦ or view it on the map ⑧. To place a waypoint in a route, see *Creating a Route* on page 88.

Edit or Delete a Waypoint

1

Press the **Menu** button and highlight *Pts of Interest* ❶. Now press the **Enter** button.

2

Highlight *My Pts of Interest* ❷ and press the **Enter** button. Note that you can search for POIs in two ways ❸:

• by Nearest   • by Alphabetic.

You can change the method by highlighting the window at the bottom of the screen and moving the joystick left or right.

3

Your POI will normally be stored in the *Default POI File* ❹. This should appear by default. Scroll down the POI list until you are highlighting the one you want ❺. Now press the **Menu** button to show the POI menu.

4

Move the cursor to the command you wish to execute. If you wish to delete a POI ❻ you will be asked to confirm this. Note that there is a *Help* section ❼ which is useful if you are unsure how to proceed when using your GPS outdoors.

You may find the **Magellan GPS File Storage System** diagram on page 82 helpful.

MAGELLAN

Creating a GoTo Route

1

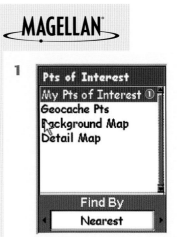

Press the **GoTo** button. You will now see the **Pts of Interest** menu. Highlight the type of POI you want to GoTo, such as *My Pts of Interest* ❶. Now press the **Enter** button.

2

Choose the method you would like to use to find a POI, for example POIs near your current position ❷, and press the **Enter** button.

3

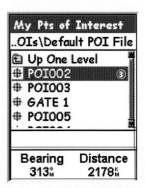

Highlight the POI you wish to navigate to ❸ and press the **Enter** button. You will be taken to the map screen to be able to navigate your GoTo route. A GoTo route does not have to be deactivated. The system will warn you if you try to enter another GoTo route.

Creating a Route

MAGELLAN

1

From the menu, select **Routes** and press the **Enter** button.

The *Default Route File* appears by default **❶**. Now highlight the *New Route* line **❷** and press the **Enter** button to start creating your route.

2

The **Create Route** screen now appears with the *Add POI* line already highlighted **❸**. Just press the **Enter** button to start adding POI to your new route. Follow the on-screen instructions to find & enter the first POI.

3

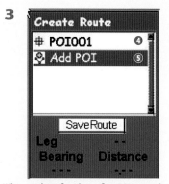

When you have found your first POI, press the **Enter** button to drop it into your new route as shown above **❹**. Repeat the process **❺** until all POIs have been entered.

NOTE: All the POI that you wish to go into your route must have been already entered into the POI database before you can start this process.

4

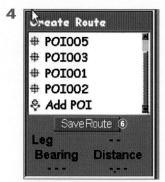

Now highlight the **Save Route** area **❻** and press the **Enter** button. You will be asked to name the route. Click on **OK** when finished. Now you will be asked where you wish to store the route (normally the *Default Route File*) confirm this and the route is saved ready to be used later.

You may find the **Magellan GPS File Storage System** diagram on page 82 helpful.

MAGELLAN

Amending a Route

1

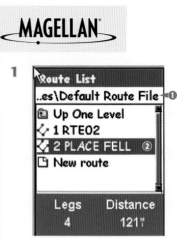

From the menu, select **Routes** and press the **Enter** button.

The *Default Route File* appears by default **❶**. Now highlight the route that you wish to amend **❷** and press the **Menu** button to get to the route menu.

2

Now highlight the *Edit Route* line **❸** and press the **Enter** button. You can see the other options available to you when working with routes.

3

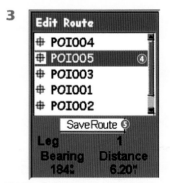

Highlight the POI you wish to amend in the route **❹** and press the **Menu** button.

4

Now select the type of amendment and press the **Enter** button. Note that *Insert POI* **❻** places a new POI (route leg) above the one that you have highlighted. When the process has been completed, highlight **Save Route ❺** and press the **Enter** button.

Navigating a Route

MAGELLAN

1

Press the **Menu** button and highlight *Pts of Interest* ❶. Now press the **Enter** button.

2

The *Default Route File* ❷ appears by default. Now highlight the route that you wish to navigate ❸ and press the **Menu** button to get to the route menu.

3

The command *Activate Route* ❹ means to 'navigate the route' and is highlighted by default, so press the **Enter** button again to start to activate the route.

Note that an 'active' route is the one being navigated.

4

To see the active route on the map screen, press the **Page** button until this is visible. If you look closely you can see that the first leg of the route being navigated is highlighted in red ❺.

You may find the **Magellan GPS File Storage System** diagram on page 82 helpful.

Stopping Navigation of a (GoTo) Route

NOTE: It is important that you 'switch off' or 'deactivate' a route after you have navigated it, otherwise your GPS will constantly be directing you to the last waypoint even if several days have passed and/or you have moved to a completely different location.

1

Press the **Menu** button and highlight *Routes* ❶. Now press the **Enter** button.

2

The *Default Route File* ❷ appears by default. Now highlight the route that you wish to deactivate ❸ and press the **Menu** button to get to the route menu.

3

The *Deactivate Route* line is highlighted by default ❹, so press the **Enter** button again to deactivate it or turn the route off.

Reversing a Route

MAGELLAN

1

From the menu, select **Routes** and press the **Enter** button.
The *Default Route File* ❶ appears by default. Now highlight the route that you wish to reverse ❷ and press the **Enter** button to see the detail of the route.

2

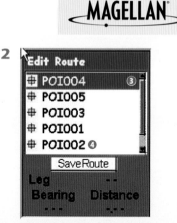

We can see that the start of this route is *POI004* ❸ and that the end of the route is *POI002* ❹. To change the direction of the route, press the **Menu** key.

3

Scroll down the list and highlight *Reverse Route* ❺ and press the **Enter** button.

4

We can see that the route has been reversed. The starting point is now *POI002* ❻ and the end or destination of the route is now *POI004* ❼. Now highlight **Save Route** ❽ and press the **Enter** button to store the reversed route.

You may find the **Magellan GPS File Storage System** diagram on page 82 helpful.

Deleting a Route

NOTE: The *Deleting a Route* command will permanently erase a route from your database. However, the points of interest that make up the route will still remain so that they can be used in other routes.

1

Menu

Pts of Interest
Routes ➀
Track Log
Adv. Features
Preferences
Weather
Help
About...

Press the **Menu** button and highlight *Routes* ➊. Now press the **Enter** button.

2

The *Default Route File* ➋ appears by default. Now highlight the route that you wish to delete ➌ and press the **Menu** button to get to the route menu.

3

Scroll down the list and highlight *Delete Route* ➍. Now press the **Enter** button. You will be asked to confirm the deletion. If you do, the route will be deleted.

Track Log: Clearing the Active Track/
Backtracking on Active Track/Saving Active Track

MAGELLAN

1

Menu
Reset Trip
Pts of Interest
Routes
Track Log ①
Adv. Features
Preferences
Weather
Help
About...

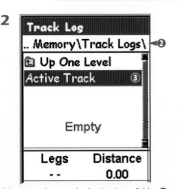

2

Track Log
.. Memory\Track Logs\ ◄②
🗀 Up One Level
Active Track ③

Empty

Legs   Distance
-- -   0.00

Press the **Menu** button and highlight **Track Log** ①. Press the **Enter** button to see the *Track Log* screen.

This screen shows us in the *Track Log* folder ② with just the active track file. There is no saved track. Compare this screen with Screen 2 on the next page where a track has been saved.
Highlight *Active Track* ③ and press the **Enter** button.

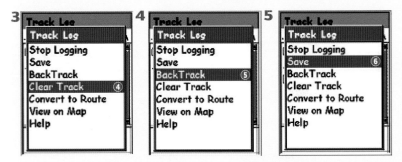

3

Track Log
Track Log
Stop Logging
Save
BackTrack
Clear Track ④
Convert to Route
View on Map
Help

4

Track Log
Track Log
Stop Logging
Save
BackTrack ⑤
Clear Track
Convert to Route
View on Map
Help

5

Track Log
Track Log
Stop Logging
Save ⑥
BackTrack
Clear Track
Convert to Route
View on Map
Help

From the **Track Log** menu you may choose to *Clear Track* ④, navigate a *BackTrack* route based on your outward journey ⑤ or *Save* the active track for use later ⑥.

You should always clear your track log before you set off. You will then just be recording today's journey.

Provided you cleared your track when you set off, you can now use the *BackTrack* feature to retrace your footsteps back to base.

You may *Save* today's journey either to navigate later or review in a digital mapping system (see *Finding and Navigating a Saved Track on page 95*).

You may find the **Magellan GPS File Storage System** diagram on page 82 helpful.

Finding & Navigating a Saved Track

NOTE: This diagram shows you how to find and navigate a track that you have already saved.
If you want to track back to base using your active track (not a saved track), look at the preceding diagram.
Track waypoints are coded *TK*, for example: *TK0004*.

1

Press the **Menu** button and highlight *Track Log* ❶. Press the **Enter** button to see the **Track Log** screen.

2

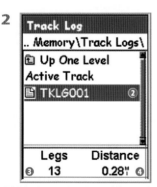

Highlight the saved track you wish to navigate ❷. You can see how many legs the track has ❸, and the overall distance of the track ❹. Now press the **Menu** button.

In this example, we can see that the saved track has been given the name *TKLG001* (Track Log Number 1).

3

- Choose *Follow Track* ❺:
  to navigate a saved track in the same direction that you travelled to create it.

- Choose *Reverse Track* ❻:
  to navigate a saved track in the opposite direction that you travelled to create it (a *BackTrack*).

Now just follow the instructions and start navigating.

05

Digital maps explained

Why would you need a digital map when a paper map has done the job for all these years and, besides, you can take a paper map with you and refer to it as required?
Well – providing you wish to remain a traditionalist that's a perfectly reasonable line to take.

Introduction

Modern times provide modern solutions. Digital maps provide the navigator with tools undreamt of before. They can be very useful as a stand-alone resource allowing you to plan routes and print maps without the need to possess a GPS. However they really come into their own when the two systems are combined and exploited to their fullest potential.

In the following chapter we try to explain exactly what digital map software can do, how it can be used in tandem with a GPS, and the benefits in both time and convenience of combining the two.

When we refer to a digital map in the GPS context, we mean an exact digital version of a paper map, such as Ordnance Survey maps used in the UK or IGN in France. The owners of the copyright of the paper maps have either produced a digital reproduction of the paper map themselves or have licensed an independent company to do so.

Digital Mapping Software

The function of any digital mapping software is to display any map that is compatible with that software and to allow the map to be used in a number of useful ways. Some of the more sophisticated software like **_Memory-Map_** will be able to display maps for use on land, sea, and air. They are written in such a way that they allow the user to overlay information, text and pictures on a digital map, and then if required transfer information either way between the map and a compatible GPS system.

You will have noticed a very important word here – _compatible_. Before you buy any GPS or mapping software, ensure that they are compatible with each other and with your PC. In addition, some of the newer digital mapping features like '3D View' and 'Fly Through' will need a PC with the specifications to make it work.

Because there is intense competition between the various brands, mapping software is in a constant process of change and catch up, which we believe is healthy for the user. It is very difficult to put a finger on one brand and say this is the best. However some are more innovative and have a track record of being first in the field with new innovations and the rest play catch up to some degree.

Like a GPS, there are some basic features that are included in all brands of mapping software, but there are subtle differences between the products that makes them more or less user friendly. However, these are the main basic features you would expect to find in most mapping software products:

expert tip

It's important to remember that the digital map itself cannot be downloaded to a GPS unless it is a computer based GPS. Only the waypoint and route data can be downloaded.

Above: Digital mapping screen images

Top and right: Working with digital mapping software

- waypoint creation and editing;
- route planning and editing;
- distance and time calculations using Naismith's Rule;
- print maps;
- transfer maps to PC;
- download waypoint and route data to your GPS from your PC;
- plot your real time position overlaid on PC or Pocket PC with GPS connected;
- review your performance by uploading track data from GPS to PC;
- save your routes and tracks on PC for review and later editing.

What Types of Digital Maps are Available?

Land-based maps

In the UK, Ordnance Survey dominates the market for maps used on land, with the most popular scale for walkers and recreational users being 1:25.000. Most digital maps for use on land in the UK are produced in these three scales:

- **1:250,000**   UK Road Maps
- **1:50,000**   Landranger Maps
- **1:25,000**   Explorer Maps

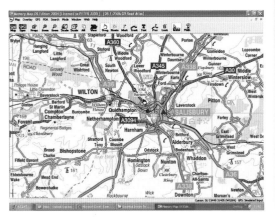

Above: A–Z Street Atlas

Left: OS 1:250,000 road map on Memory Map

For more information on all aspects of the UK grid system and maps, visit www.ordnancesurvey.co.uk. It has a particularly good section for the younger user.

Another UK mapmaker is **_Harvey Maps_**. Their method of displaying contour information above the fell wall is very popular with orienteers and walkers. Visit www.harveymaps.co.uk for more information.

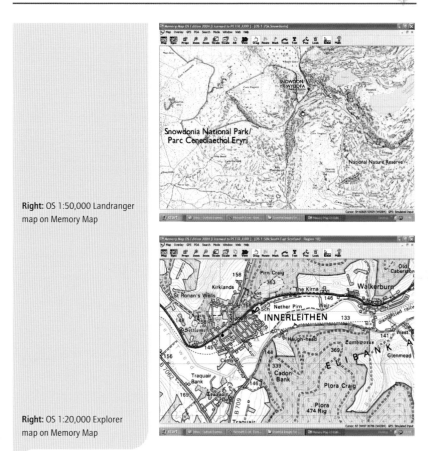

Right: OS 1:50,000 Landranger map on Memory Map

Right: OS 1:20,000 Explorer map on Memory Map

Street Maps

A–Z Maps first appeared in 1936 and are popular with anyone wishing to make their way around large cities and urban areas. They are based on Ordnance Survey maps of assorted scales and are available in both black and white and colour. A–Z publishes 340 titles including Street Maps and Atlases.

A–Z has been producing digital maps since 1996, and the maps contain a huge amount of information. For instance the Greater London version contains an index of 90,000 streets and places of interest. This type of product is ideal for the person who needs to find street locations, such as delivery or sales personnel. For more information about A–Z and its products, visit www.a-zmaps.co.uk.

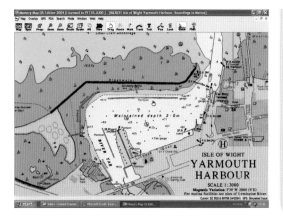

Above: A MapTech Marine digital chart for sailors
Left: MapTech Marine nautical chart on Memory-Map

Marine Charts

Walkers, bikers and other road users are not the only ones to see the benefits of combining GPS and digital mapping. Sailors were amongst the first users of GPS navigation. To meet this demand, there is once again a good choice of mapping available.

One of the main reasons Britain developed to become one of the world's leading maritime powers was the quality of our charts. For all you need to know about paper and digital charts for the mariner go to www.hydro.gov.uk.

MapTech Marine Software is the leading supplier of digital charts that can be used with a handheld GPS. Those who don't wish to use a laptop at sea could combine a Pocket PC and GPS. For more information on MapTech software visit www.memory-map.co.uk. Both leading GPS manufacturers can supply software for maritime use.

Aviation Charts

The aviation industry is a big user of GPS systems in all its forms. For the individual user there are digital charts that contain viewable and printable information on airports, aerodromes and heliports throughout the UK.

CAA Charts are available in 1:500,000 and 1:250,000 VFR Charts for use with ***Memory-Map*** software.

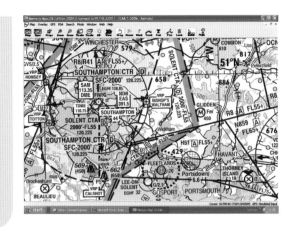

Right: CAA aviation chart on Memory-Map

Worldwide Digital Maps

There are digital maps available for many countries in the world. A growing trend is for travellers to pre-plan their routes and expeditions in the comfort of their armchair and on the PC. Hence the growth in digital maps available on CD and DVD.

Many of the popular tourist destinations and developed countries of the world have digital maps and charts and their licensing authority or software developer will have agency arrangements to distribute their products worldwide. In the past most maps in the world have been distributed within the book trade, so here is the most likely place to find worldwide digital maps.

There are a number of specialist companies that specialise in maps in the UK like Stanfords with branches in London, Bristol, and Manchester www.stanfords.co.uk, The Penrith Map Room in Cumbria, www.penrithmaproom.co.uk and Cordee, www.cordee.co.uk/maps.

Which Software Do You Buy?

Most mapping software will perform the basic functions of route/waypoint creation and will allow transfer of data to GPS. However each product will present these functions in a different way with varying levels of user friendliness. In addition to the basics there are interesting map features like 3D View and Fly Through which, when combined with Aerial View, take the study of maps to a new level. Although the more sophisticated of these features do increase the price, they really do increase the interest and fun you can have.

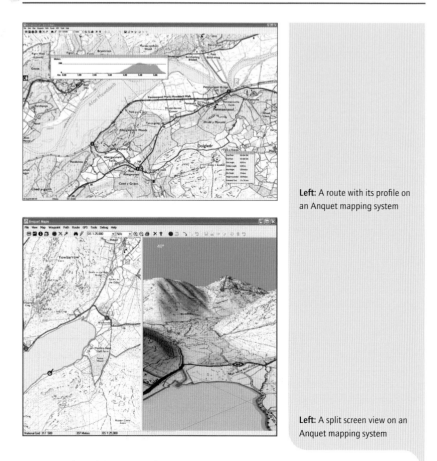

Left: A route with its profile on an Anquet mapping system

Left: A split screen view on an Anquet mapping system

A major part of the cost of any mapping software is the license to use the map itself from the owner of the copyright. In the UK this is the Ordnance Survey.

When buying digital maps you need to decide on the features you need and make sure that the operation of the system is as user-friendly as possible. If you are interested in more than a basic system, you will want to assure yourself that the product you are thinking of investing in is a leader in technical development and not a laggard. Whatever software you are considering, you also need to ensure that your computer is powerful enough to run it. One way of getting information about this is to ask friends who may have already bought into digital mapping.

Right: 3D view of O.S. Explorer mapping on an Anquet mapping system

Your retailer should also be able to give you good advice on which software to purchase. These days, many retail stores have demonstration units so you can see what these systems are capable of. They should be able to supply you with a free trial disk. The alternative is, either to go online and visit the website of the relevant system where you will be able to access sample software, maps, and in some cases download a demo or see a video, or contact them direct for a free trial disk.

Narrowing the choice
Do you buy mapping in small or large chunks and which scale do you buy? As the end user this is a very personal decision and will almost certainly be led by your own preferences. It is possible to get much larger chunks of mapping at 1:50,000 scale at a reasonable cost than at 1:25,000 scale, so perhaps one way is to obtain wide cover at 1:50,000 and then focus on areas where you need more detail in 1:25,000.

Most suppliers of software have a wide variety of mapping on offer. For example, mapping that covers specific areas such as National Parks and Trails, or options to buy mapping at a scale and area of your choice based on your home or postcode. Our advice is to shop around and, once again, make sure you are quite sure of your requirements before you purchase.

The Main Suppliers of Mapping Software in the UK

There are four main suppliers of software (at the time of going to press), all of whom are licensed partners of Ordnance Survey, although in the future we think there will be other players entering the market. We believe there is healthy competition in the software market which works in the favour of the consumer, unlike the hardware market (GPS), where one supplier dominates with only one other company as realistic competition.

As an indication of the growth of digital mapping software, few of these mapping companies were even trading before 2000.

Anquet Technology
Anquet is a British software development house specialising in mapping software for the leisure market. Their products include everything you would expect in the way of features, including 3D View, Fly Through, and Aerial View options. They also are one of the few companies to feature Harvey maps.

Anquet is in the market top two with a wide following of satisfied users.

Website: www.anquet.co.uk   Tel: 0870 990 9395
By post: **Anquet Technology**, Four Seasons House, 102B Woodstock Rd, Witney, Oxfordshire, OX28 1DZ.

Memory-Map
Privately owned and established in July 2000, *Memory-Map* has offices in the UK and in the US. They supply navigation software to the recreation, aviation and marine markets. They have been consistently at the forefront of innovation and marketing and are seen as the market leader.

e x p e r t   t i p

Before you buy!
Like any software you purchase, once you have opened the package it's yours. No one will contemplate refunds on software just because it doesn't work with your GPS or PC or is the wrong map scale. Remember that not all mapping software is compatible with all models of GPS and vice versa, so do your homework before you buy. In the long run it could save you time, effort and money.

Their software contains all the features you could expect. In addition they have strong links with Navman, and specialise in software for the growing pocket PC market. They have a growing worldwide product base, with maps available for Canada, USA, and Europe.

Website: www.memory-map.co.uk
Tel: 0870 740 9040
By post: **Memory-Map Europe**, Unit 3–4 Mars House, Calleva Park, Aldermaston, RG7 8JA

Fugawi

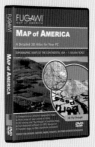

A Canadian company whose navigation products offer affordable, feature-packed software that locates your exact position on land or sea. FUGAWI offers an incredible variety of world maps and has topographic maps for many parts of the world, as well as street maps for Europe, Canada, the United States and South Africa. Marine charts are available for most of the world's waters. They offer a wide range of Ordnance Survey options at reasonable prices.

Fugawi offers no frills software with a good library of worldwide maps.

Website: www.fugawi.com
International Tel. From UK: 011 – 416 – 920 – 9300
By post: **Northport Systems Inc**, 95 St Clair Ave West, Suite 1406, Toronto, Ontario, Canada. M4V 1N6

Tracklogs

A British company based in Derbyshire who have developed their own software. In addition, they are an online retailer that specialise in digital mapping applications for recreational users. Relatively new to the market, they have been quite innovative in their approach to packaging their software, Internet sales and trails.

Website: www.tracklogs.co.uk   Tel: 01298 872537
By post: **Tracklogs**, The Old Dairy, Great Hucklow, Derbyshire, SK17 8RG

Getting Started and Connecting to your PC

GPS manufacturers and digital mapping companies receive more customer queries about GPS/PC connection problems than all the rest put together. The task of connecting to your PC usually comes when the product is new to the user and patience is at a premium. Take your time and read the section on connection to a PC in the GPS owner's manual before you start.

Left: Making the GPS/ PC connection

Getting Started

OK – so you've opened the box, now what? Having loaded the software onto your PC, you will have to register and obtain a license key to enable the product. This procedure is a necessary protection to protect the supplier from fraud. Your individual license key will unlock and enable certain features like printing and GPS and PDA links. The easiest way to register is online. However there will be arrangements to register by phone if you prefer.

At this stage you will probably be asked to sign up for a newsletter. This is usually worth doing on the basis you will be kept informed about any software updates and new product releases.

Above: An RS232 serial port

e x p e r t   t i p

If you have connection problems in the future, check through the 9 Steps on page 110 as the COM Port number being used by your mapping system may have changed.

Mapping software is always in a process of being updated. This is to iron out software glitches, update new GPS models as they come on stream and upgrade and add new features to the software. It is therefore worth making sure that from day one you work with the latest version. You will find details of the version you are using in the *Help* menu. Armed with this information, go online to check if there are any updates available for you to download. The alternative to an update online is to use an upgrade disk.

Technical support is available in several forms: product guide and help menu in the software; dedicated help lines; frequently asked questions (FAQs) and user forums on the supplier's website. If you are stuck and need help, then the FAQs and user forums are well worth a visit, as you can be sure you are not the first person with that question. The answer to your problem could well be there and you won't have to wait for the office to open to resolve your problem.

GETTING STARTED & CONNECTING TO YOUR PC ▼

Connecting to your PC

In this section we try to remove some of the mystique surrounding this issue by explaining how to successfully make the GPS/PC connection. There are three steps to completing this task:

Step 1

Install your mapping system and ensure you have the latest upgrade. The installation of software and updates is generally quite straightforward. Care should be taken to follow the manufacturer's instructions. Some products require an unlock code or license key – a device to prevent copying of the software.

Step 2

Buy the correct cable(s) and drivers to link the two then correctly install/link them together. Cables come either as part of the GPS package or have to be bought as an accessory. In either case you have to ensure that you have the correct connection for your PC. Each manufacturer has developed its own cable system to connect a GPS to a computer. The end that connects to your GPS will have a uniquely shaped fitting to try to ensure that you buy it from them. Given the model, your manufacturer or retailer will sell you a compatible cable.

The other end of the cable is either a standard serial (RS232) female connector or, with the latest generation of GPS, a USB connection.

Many modern PCs and laptops do not have RS232 interfaces as they rely on the faster USB system. This presents a problem for these owners, as they must buy an extra cable to be able to convert the original RS232 to a USB connector to be able to plug it into their computer. These are called USB to RS232 converter cables and come with their own driver software. These can be bought from the manufacturers (expensive) or over the Internet (much cheaper).

Above: 2 USB ports

Be very careful if you buy a non-branded product as it may not work correctly. Always buy from a reputable source.

Step 3
Ensure you create the correct data pathway between GPS and PC to enable them to talk to each other. On leaving the factory your GPS will be set to the default setting – GARMIN for **Garmins** and MAGELLAN for **Magellans**. Although there are other settings, the need to switch to one of them is most unusual. Our advice therefore is do not change the default interface settings unless you either know what you are doing, or have sought professional advice. If you are unsure, try the GPS manufacturer's or the digital map manufacturer's website first for information.

Types of connections
Serial Port Connection
If you connect your GPS directly to a serial port, you will need to set your digital mapping system to COM1 in GPS Setup. If COM port 1 is already being used by another device, then you may have difficulties. If you cannot resolve this yourself, you may have to consult a computer specialist.

Connection via a USB to RS232 Converter Cable
If you connect to a USB port with a USB to RS232 converter cable, the COM setting could be any number between from 2 upwards depending on the other equipment you have connected. Although you can find the correct port number by trial and error, you may find the following approach easier:

1 Plug your cable into the computer and switch on the GPS receiver.
2 Go into the 'Control Panel'. Depending on the version of *Microsoft*® *Windows*® you have, this is usually found from the Start Menu.
3 If you cannot find it, go into the Help system and find out where to locate it.

4 Click on System, then Hardware, then Device Manager, then Ports (COM and LPT).

5 Now click on the '+' symbol to reveal the different types of ports you have.

6 Look for the 'Serial on USB Port' or 'USB Port' or something similar.

7 This will show which COM port is currently being used – for example (COM4).

8 Now close down the various windows you have opened and get back to your digital mapping system.

9 Enter the COM port number into your digital mapping system that your computer is using for the USB connection.

expert tip

Finding your way around digital map software
One good way to find out what everything does is to work your way along the tool bar, opening each menu and submenu and just experiment by seeing what options are available to you. Use the help system to get extra information when you need it. If you get really stuck then there will be technical support available either online or on a dedicated support line.

Connection via a USB Cable

Having installed the driver software correctly all you need to do here is connect up your GPS to the PC via any one of the USB ports and set your digital mapping system to 'USB'.

GETTING STARTED & CONNECTING TO YOUR PC

T A S K

Setting up your digital mapping software to work with your GPS.

1. Open your mapping software system.
2. Connect your GPS to its cable.

If you have a serial port and serial cable:
3. connect the other end of the cable to the appropriate port on your PC;
4. set your GPS setting in your mapping software to 'COM 1';
5. transfer data to and from your GPS using the correct commands depending on your mapping software.

If you have a USB to RS232 converter cable –
Having correctly installed the driver software:
3. connect the loose end of the GPS cable to the converter cable and connect the other end of the cable to the appropriate port on your PC;
4. follow the instructions given earlier in this chapter to locate the correct COM port number;
5. enter the correct COM port number into the GPS settings area of your mapping software;
6. transfer data to and from your GPS using the correct commands depending on your mapping software.

If you have a USB GPS device and USB cable –
Having correctly installed the driver software:
3. connect the other end of the cable to the appropriate port on your PC;
4. set the GPS setting in your mapping software to USB;
5. transfer data to and from your GPS using the correct commands depending on your mapping software.

06

Bringing it all together

In this section we have put
together some useful hints, tips,
and information that will not only
enable you to stay safe in the hills,
but help you get the best from
your GPS and mapping software at
home and abroad.

Introduction

A lot of the fun of any journey is in the planning and preparation. Good planning will add to that feeling of confidence while you are out there and will add to your safety. Whatever method of navigation you use, the basic principles remain the same.

Route Planning Basics with Paper Maps

The key considerations when planning any route will be:

- the ability and fitness of your group;
- the time and daylight available (allow a safety margin);
- the distance and terrain you plan to cover;
- the weather forecast.

Don't bite off more than you can chew! Granny might not be able to make it up Snowdon in two hours, but she might quite like a stroll along the banks of the Thames. Tailor your route to your personal abilities when alone, otherwise think about the abilities of your group. Many a potential walker has been put off by someone's over ambitious route planning.

Consider the skills and experience of both you and your group. Is your route feasible? How many hours of daylight do you have? Is it too far for the time you have allowed? Have you been too ambitious? Is there time built in for breaks and to enjoy the views?

Remember it takes longer to climb up than come down, so when calculating a time estimate for your route you will need to build in an allowance for any ascent involved in your expedition. Estimating distance and time by traditional methods can be tricky, however even rough estimations of this basic information should help you to plan a safe route.

Try using this rough 'rule of thumb' to estimate the time required to cover a distance when walking at a reasonable pace. Divide the total distance by 3km per hour and then add 10 minutes for every 100m of ascent.

Example:
You plan to visit a local beauty spot which is approx 9km away. The height gain is 200m.

Distance	(9km ÷ 3km per hour)	3 hours
Ascent	(200m ÷ 100m = 2×10 minutes)	20mins
Total time required		**3 hrs 20mins**

T A S K :

Using the following distances and height gains, calculate an estimate of time using the formula above:

- Distance 12km – Height Gain 400m
- Distance 5km – Height Gain 900m
- Distance 15km – Height Gain 600m

To obtain a rough estimate of distance from a paper map, simply count the number of grid squares your route passes through. More accuracy can be obtained by using a Romer Scale. Counting the contour lines on the map is the key to estimating height gain. In upland areas every line is an increase in height of 10m. Every fifth line is made thicker to make counting easier. It's worth noting that heights are always marked going uphill, streams are usually in valleys, water always runs downhill and the closer the contour lines the steeper the climb or descent.

Putting together a Route Plan

To take a stroll from the pub to the church might just require a simple route with the minimum of detail. However an excursion into the Scottish mountains would probably need detailed route planning. In essence we need to work out the best line of travel between A and B dependent on our mode of transport, and then think about significant turns and markers on the way. Why do we need all this information? To make the task of navigation in the field easier and less stressful!

Having decided on your destination, now is the time to consult the map! Make notes on your route such as the footpaths you intend to follow. Then work out distance, height gain/loss together with an estimate of time and then apply the key basic considerations. If you feel your route meets your criteria you can proceed to add some detail to your plan.

Navigation in the field becomes easier the more detail or confirmation points we have. Generally these points in a route are referred to as waypoints. A waypoint is a position on the ground expressed as a grid reference. Add waypoints together and you create a route.

When creating a waypoint it's usually fairly straightforward where to place it. Try and use a position on the map that is also going to be significant on the ground, like a footbridge or a building – better still if your building has a house name. There's nothing more reassuring, when you're not quite sure where you are, than to be able to confirm your position with a positive reference to an easily confirmed waypoint, such as Askham Church for instance:

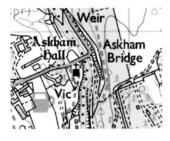

Askham Church as shown on the map *(left)* **and on the ground** *(right).*

All that is required now is to list your selected waypoints in the order you wish to follow them to form a **Route**. Each section between two waypoints in a route is generally referred to as a **Leg**. The waypoint list is called a **Route Card**. Many walkers will carry one with them as a guide to where significant turns and confirmation points are on the route.

A simple route card for this route with two legs from the village pub to the church might look like this:

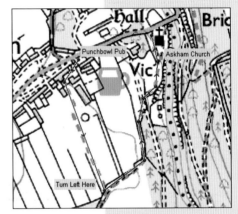

Above: Pub to Church Route

Waypoint Name	Grid Reference	Notes
Pub	NY 516/238	Turn left (SW) from pub after lunch
Turn	NY 516/235	Turn left (NE) here
Church	NY 518/248	Parish Church

Waypoints in a Route

A book could be written on this subject alone. Waypoint placement can and should vary according to your mode of transport and method of navigation. Taking these influences into consideration, deciding where to place waypoints in a route can be critical to ensuring a safe arrival at your destination.

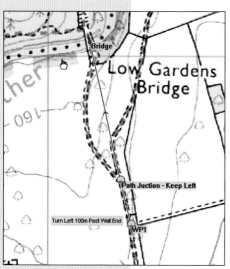

Above: Bridge Route

When it comes to **Decision Points** such as the path junction shown in the diagram for instance, the more information to hand, the easier it will be to stay on course.

To give us the maximum navigation information on the first leg of this route we have created **WP1** at the wall corner (to give us a reference point). We have worked out that the distance from **WP1** to the path junction is approximately 100m (about 65 double paces) and that on arrival at the path junction we need to keep to the left path and expect that in about 450m (about 290 double paces) we will arrive at the bridge. In theory, one would need to do this type of exercise for every leg of any route – quite a laborious process you will agree.

Using a GPS with mapping software can really make life easy when it comes to route planning, although with a GPS we would place waypoints using slightly different principles. This is a subject we will explore later in this chapter.

Navigating a Route

When you have created, planned and put together your route you've done the hard work. There's nothing difficult about navigating a route provided you follow a few simple rules:

- fix your position on the map at the beginning of your walk;
- 'set the map' so that your route line runs ahead of you
  (from bottom to top of your map);
- look at your map to see what might be the next significant point en route that might confirm your location as you move forward;
- move from one known position to the next so it's more difficult to get lost.

Traditional Route Planning Reviewed

All the basic principles discussed in the notes above apply whichever method of navigation you choose to use. This leaves the door open for us to explore the advantages that digital mapping software can provide.

If you have done the exercises earlier in the book you will probably agree that manual waypoint and route creation with a map or with a GPS can be quite a laborious and error prone business.

Imagine if instead of all the tedious manual waypoint creation work, all you had to do to create a waypoint was simply one click of your mouse. **Interested? Then read on!**

The key to transforming both these tasks from chores into interesting and relatively error free activity is to buy into one of the easy to use digital mapping systems on the market, as described in the previous chapter *Digital Maps Explained*.

Route Planning with a Digital Mapping System

It's not necessary to be a GPS owner to tap into the many advantages of owning a digital mapping system. Even without a GPS you can still create waypoints and plan routes (and much more).

A great feature of many mapping systems is that wherever you rest your cursor on the map you will see a position fix displayed as a 10-figure grid reference with the elevation shown at that point. Both the position format and map units can be altered to suit your requirements.

In most mapping systems you can now use real colour maps like Ordnance Survey Landranger™ and Explorer™ on your PC, laptop, or pocket PC. To add waypoints and routes just click on the map. You can even draw a track freehand. Every route will calculate leg distances, compass bearings, total journey length and time. All waypoints, routes and tracks created can be saved for later use. Route cards and maps with the route displayed can be seen and printed.

You can display hill profiles and visualise the terrain around your routes and tracks in 3D. With the aerial photography view (available on some maps), you can see, 'fly-through' movies of your routes and tracks.

In addition some systems will allow you to access sites on the Internet, such as Walkingworld, directly through the mapping system. You can then download routes

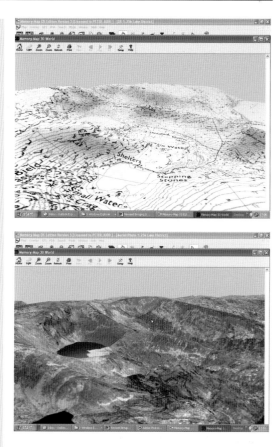

Right: 3D View of High Street in the Lakes

Right: 3D Aerial View of High Street in the Lakes. Footpaths on the high fells show up well in the aerial view

complete with GPS waypoints and print off paper copies of your routes, waypoints and tracks for use in the field.

Save and Share your Routes and Tracks

Mapping software will allow you to save any routes or tracks you have created for future use. This is an extremely useful planning tool, especially when combined with the overlay manager – an easy to use route, track and waypoint manager.

PRINTING MAPS

In most systems you can choose to:
- **print** at the scale of your choice;
- **draw** grid lines and add labels;
- **choose** paper size and orientation;
- **alter** margins and preview;
- **customise** your printing (for longer routes);
- **add** detailed text to your maps;

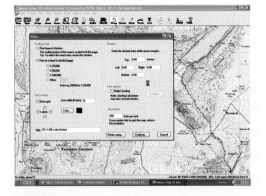

- **print** your route card detailing waypoints, compass bearings, distances, and grid co-ordinates, and include notes & photos;
- **print** maps showing 3D terrain on an accurate 2D scale map, making it easy to interpret contour lines.

Left: Choose your print options in Memory-Map V5

Left: Print out a Route Card with Route Profile and embedded images as seen in Memory-Map V5

expert tip

To protect your printed maps we recommend that you either laminate them or use waterproof paper.

Sharing Data

Having saved your data to your PC, it can easily be managed and, usefully, you can share your data with friends provided they are using a compatible mapping system. As overlay files only transfer the co-ordinates, a typical file might be under 50Kb so it is easily transferable by e-mail without broadband.

Right: *Save As* screen

Route Planning with a Digital Mapping System and a GPS

We have already reviewed some of the advantages of using a digital mapping even if you don't possess a GPS. If you do have a digital mapping system and a GPS then you have the very powerful and time saving bonus of being able to upload waypoints and routes straight into your GPS and download tracks from your GPS back into your mapping system.

In this section we have put together some useful hints, tips and information that should not only assist you in staying safe in the hills, but also help you get the best from your GPS and mapping software both at home and abroad. Although most of the information is common sense, we believe there that there are subtle differences in the way you navigate when you add GPS into the equation and learn to use the features inherent in the unit.

Left: Add Hotspots to your Routes

Waypoint Placement with a GPS

Where you place each waypoint is crucial when planning a GPS route. It can make the difference between safely negotiating a turn and missing the turn so possibly placing yourself in a dangerous situation.

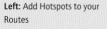

Let's go back to our route planning task used previously in this chapter to illustrate a few important points relative to route planning and waypoint placement with GPS in mind.

The Low Bridge Path diagram opposite illustrates possible GPS waypoints to be used in a route we wish to create to take us on foot to the bridge.

The crux of the problem is the GPS's circle of accuracy. When in **Route** mode, your GPS is doing a series of **GoTos** and could move on to the next waypoint in the route anywhere within its accuracy circle. This could be either before or after the waypoint. In theory you could be more than 30m before or after a waypoint when it moves on to navigate to the next one in the route.

Using our illustration, where should you place waypoints in the vicinity of the footpath junction to make sure you are guided by the GPS onto the correct path? Think about this and come up with your solution before you read on.

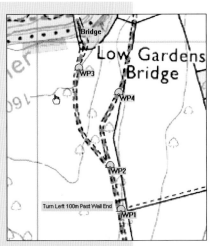

Above: Low Bridge Path

WAYPOINT PLACEMENT WITH A GPS

METHOD 1

If we were to create our route using the waypoints on offer in the following order **WP1 → WP2 → Bridge**. Our GPS would, after passing through the circle of accuracy at **WP1**, lock onto **WP2**. On arrival at **WP2** the GPS may not yet have locked onto the next waypoint (**Bridge**). As we have no accurate bearing at this point, we may take the wrong path towards **WP4** until we passed through the circle of accuracy of **WP2** and our GPS then locked onto **Bridge**. Hopefully at this point we would realise our error and be able to retrace our steps to **WP2** and so regain the correct path to **Bridge**.

METHOD 2

What if we were to use some of the waypoints in the diagram in the following order **WP1 → WP3 → Bridge**? How would our GPS navigate us?

As we get close to **WP1** a modern GPS should tell us we have a turn coming up although many GPS do not have this feature. Then when we pass through the circle of accuracy of **WP1** the GPS should lock onto **WP3** and give a dynamic bearing to that position. This would have the effect of clearly pointing us to the left at the path junction towards **WP3**. We could even attach a message to **WP1** saying 'Turn left in 80m'. Importantly **WP2** would still be visible on our map screen, giving us confirmation at that point we were at the path junction.

This illustrates two ways of creating a route from **WP1** to **Bridge**. The second method uses the full capabilities of a GPS whilst the other could allow you to make an error of judgement and waste time retracing your steps.

e x p e r t   t i p

Important information for bike and car users!

50/100m is soon covered in a car or on a bike. So when route planning for a vehicle or mountain bike then, to allow for the speed you are travelling, place waypoints further back from the turning point. Set the proximity alarm to sound further away from each waypoint, either from within your GPS (dependent on model) or from within your digital mapping system (if you use one).

This is only one way we could use GPS features to improve our route planning skills with the GPS and mapping tools on offer – we are sure that with a little forethought you will be able to find many other solutions to navigation problems.

Tips on route planning with GPS in mind

- Always include a waypoint at the start of your route as your GPS will always skip the first waypoint and navigate you to the second waypoint in your route.
- Use the minimum number of waypoints in your route. In general terms, the more tricky the terrain the more waypoints you should use.
- Wherever possible use waypoints that are a distance apart that is greater than the typical circle of accuracy (30m without WAAS/ EGNOS).
- Record each waypoint on paper (such as a route card produced by a digital mapping system) for reference on route and for lodging with someone back at base.
- Think about an escape route(s) for emergencies and, wherever possible, put the route (even a **GoTo**) into your GPS before you set off.
- Place waypoints at key decision points in your route, but not exactly at path or road junctions. Place them about 100m before and after the decision point. The first waypoint will remind you that you are nearly there whilst the one afterwards will 'pull you' onto the right route.
- Waypoints placed too close to each other might confuse your GPS.
- Linear routes can be reversed.

e x p e r t   t i p

Waypoint placement is a skill and will affect the accuracy of the bearing your GPS is giving you. Correct waypoint placement should ensure that you make turns at the correct places.

Getting the best out of the Route function

Unless you want to know the area of a piece of land, it is not generally a good idea to create a circular route. (This is a route where the start and end waypoints are the same). The reason for this is that sometimes a GPS can become confused and 'think' that it has already reached its destination as soon as it starts to navigate.

The best approach is to create a 'tight horseshoe' route where the start and end waypoints are very close together but not the same. This type of route would get you back to base without any confusion.

If your route out and back are very close – for example out along one bank of a small river and back along the other – again your GPS may get confused. The reason for this is that the waypoints on each side of the river are close enough to each other to be within the GPS' circle of accuracy. The GPS (being just a 'stupid' computer) may then mistakenly think that you have reached the waypoint on the opposite side of the river even though you are actually on the outbound legs of your route.

To get round this problem, create two separate routes – one outbound and the other inbound. Now there can be no confusion. If you own a GPS that is limited to just one route, you will have to do a **GoTo** to get past the problem area.

Having created a route, if you have a digital mapping system, you could:

- Check your route profile – plan to get the 'ups' done in the first part of the day.
- Look at your route properties – the total route distance and how long it will take you. You can adjust the elements of Naismith's Rule to suit your speed.
- Print off a copy of the map showing both the route and escape route to the same scale as your paper map if possible.
- Print off two copies of the route cards (route and escape route) and give one to someone who will know if you fail to return (such as a partner or B&B owner).
- Save the routes to a map data folder on your PC and take a back-up.

When you get back you can review your performance against your plan.

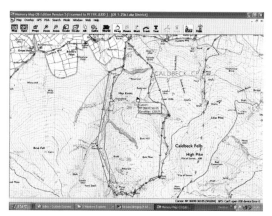

Right: Viewing both route and track overlays together allows you to review your performance

Learning Tasks

The following tasks will allow you to practise your route planning skills whilst taking some of the points raised in this chapter into consideration. To be able to get the maximum benefit from the exercise, and be able to compare the requirements of route planning firstly with a paper map and then with a digital mapping systems, you will need maps of the same area preferably at the same scale.

T A S K   1 :

Route creation using a Paper Map.

Imagine you are taking a group of friends and their children on a walk tomorrow. As group leader, you have volunteered to prepare the route and provide everyone taking part with the fullest details of the proposed outing.

Your route should be about 10km long and must be within the capabilities of all taking part. Please bear in mind that there is only a time window for the walk of 5 hours and the weather forecast is for strong northerly winds and sunny spells with a maximum temperature in the valleys of 12°C and 2°C at 3000 feet.

Produce a route plan for the group to include map, route card, and the following information:

- Start point with grid reference
- Waypoint details including grid references – with navigation notes if required
- Details of timings – distance – and height gain for the route.
- Proposal for the stopping point for lunch and the time allowed.

T A S K   2 :

Route creation using a Digital Mapping System.

Now complete the same task on your favourite mapping system.
How do the two tasks compare?

C H E C K   Y O U R   L E A R N I N G

1. Which is not a key consideration when planning a walking route:
a) The height gain over the walk.
b) Time of sunset.
c) The age of the oldest person in the group.

2. Using the rough 'rule of thumb' to estimate time to cover distance, how many minutes should you add for each 100m of ascent?
a) 5
b) 10
c) 15

3. In upland areas on a 1:25,000 Explorer map, what is the distance between each contour line?
a) 10m
b) 25m
c) 50m

4. Which way should a map be orientated?
a) Tightly folded to stop it being caught by the wind
b) Upward so you can read it easily whilst looking ahead
c) With the route running ahead of you

5. Which of the following would you not expect a digital map system to do?
a) Add text boxes to your digital maps
b) Advise the best place to stop for a break
c) Print maps at the same scale as your paper map

6. Where should you not usually place a waypoint when designing a route with a GPS?
a) At a decision point
b) About 100m before a decision point
c) About 30m before a decision point

The answers can be found on page 165.

Be Prepared Before You Set Off

Batteries

We all do it – set off without checking the battery status before we leave, then the batteries run out. The chances are you've forgotten to take spares, giving credence to all those Luddites who will happily tell you your unit won't work without batteries.

Your safety may depend on your GPS so charged batteries are vital. On average you can expect about 12–15 hours of use from a new set of alkaline batteries. It's good practise to carry at least one spare set and test all your batteries before you go on a trip. The last thing you need to be doing is to have to change your batteries on a wet and windy day.

GPS backlighting is a heavy user of battery power. Use with care and set the backlight timer function if your GPS has one. GPS electronic compass/altimeter features are also battery drainers. Switch them off until you need them.

If you use rechargeable batteries, Ni-MH are preferable as they have no memory and can be safely recharged even when not fully discharged. Choose the highest mAh rating you can find. Batteries rated at less than about 1800 mAh will usually give poor performance relative to an alkaline battery. Rechargeable batteries tend to power out without much warning.

Stored data is not lost when you change the batteries, provided the GPS is switched off first.

There is a battery drain even when the GPS is switched off so, provided your GPS is a modern type with a flash memory, take the batteries out if you are not going to use your GPS for a long time.

Some GPS have a battery type setting. If there is a setting option, make sure this is set correctly to get an accurate reading on the battery life indicator.

Before leaving home – check that you have:

- a paper map for entire planned walk including a route card;
- a compass with a Romer scale (integral or separate);
- spare batteries that you have checked recently.

e x p e r t   t i p

If possible, check the power left in your batteries at the outdoor temperature you will be walking in. Checking them in a warm room may be very misleading.

Before moving off – preparation

Most of us spend several minutes at the beginning of each journey preparing our kit and putting our boots on. Why not use that time to good advantage?

Put your GPS on the roof of the car or somewhere flat and give it time to obtain a good position fix whilst you're getting ready. Allow your GPS time to settle before moving off, and check the position given by the GPS against a map. Also check the status of your batteries and change them now if necessary.

Clear your track log if you wish to create a *TracBack* or *BackTrack* or review your track log at the end of the day. Reset your trip computer if you wish to record your day's performance, such as distance, speed and so on. If you are not immediately navigating a route, mark your starting position, name it *Car/Start* so that you have a reference point.

On the walk

Check your position regularly. Be aware of the ground around you as you go, path junctions, boundaries, footbridges, streams and so on can all help to confirm your position.

On arrival at a waypoint in a route

Look and listen for your proximity alarm (if you have one) and keep moving on to your next waypoint in the route. Check whether your GPS has advanced to navigate you to the next waypoint. If not, check your position with your map/plot screen and move on. Always stay aware of where you are, and check your map at key points on the route.

e x p e r t   t i p

If you wish to navigate to a precise position then do a **GoTo**. It will be the most accurate way to pin point any one spot. Ideal for Geocaching!

On arrival at your destination (or on a GoTo)

Look or listen for your proximity alarm (if you have one). If you can see your destination then your GPS has done its job. Stop and allow your GPS to settle and you

Left: Back to base at the YHA Ambleside

will see your position accuracy improve. If necessary, check your position with your map.

Get out there and have a great day and enjoy the views. Pre-planning will ensure you have a more relaxed trip.

Below: Getting there!

Right: I'm glad I brought my GPS!

Staying Safe with your GPS

A GPS is an aid to navigation but not a substitute for a map and compass. You should be safer with all three than with just the two.

Become used to using your GPS in good weather before you have to rely on it in bad. Get used to using the **Mark** function so you can record your position in an emergency.

You will get the best signal when you hold a GPS properly. Look at the specifications in your manual to see what type of aerial your GPS has. If it has a quadrifilar helix aerial, hold it vertically. If it has a patch aerial, hold it horizontally. Holding your GPS higher by holding your arm up can help to get a better fix.

If you need to get to safety quickly, navigate a pre-entered escape route or create a *TracBack* route (**Garmin** – *see page 81*) or *Backtrack* route (**Magellan** – *see page 94*) from your track log. You could also consider using a **GoTo** to a place of safety or reversing your route.

Use the latest GPS software

Check on the GPS manufacturer's website regularly to see if there is a GPS software upgrade available for your model – *see the diagram overleaf*. Some sites will allow you to register to get upgrades automatically. Upgrades may improve the way the software works, may provide extra map data and position formats and may add extra features to your GPS.

Checking the Software Version

≋GARMIN.

1

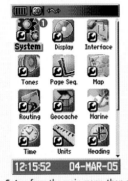

Choose **Setup** from the main menu, then choose **System ❶** and press **Enter**.

2

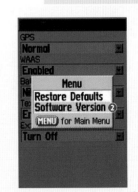

With the **System** screen showing, press the **Menu** button and highlight *Software Version* **❷**. Press **Enter**.

3

The software version currently loaded will be displayed together with the identification number of the GPS **❸**.

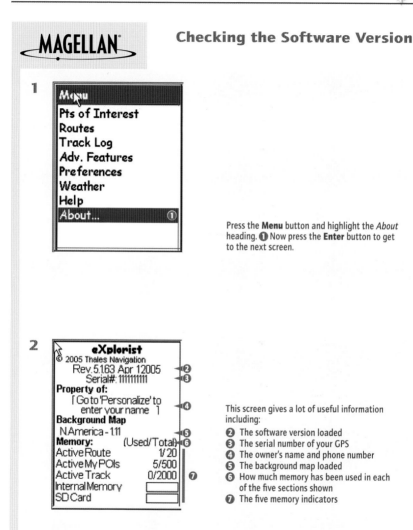

Checking the Software Version

1

Menu
Pts of Interest
Routes
Track Log
Adv. Features
Preferences
Weather
Help
About...   ❶

Press the **Menu** button and highlight the *About* heading. ❶ Now press the **Enter** button to get to the next screen.

2

eXplorist
© 2005 Thales Navigation
Rev. 5.1.63 Apr 12 2005   ❷
Serial#: 111111111   ❸
Property of:
[Go to 'Personalize' to
  enter your name]   ❹
Background Map
N.America - 1.11   ❺
Memory: (Used/Total) ❻
Active Route   1/ 20
Active My POIs   5/500
Active Track   0/2000   ❼
Internal Memory
SD Card

This screen gives a lot of useful information including:

❷ The software version loaded
❸ The serial number of your GPS
❹ The owner's name and phone number
❺ The background map loaded
❻ How much memory has been used in each of the five sections shown
❼ The five memory indicators

CHECK YOUR LEARNING

1. What should you do before you set out?
   a) Check batteries
   b) Do a GoTo
   c) Create a track log

2. Why should you allow your GPS to settle before moving off?
   a) The batteries will last longer
   b) The track log will be updated before you start moving
   c) You will get a more accurate position

3. Why is it a good idea to check an initial position fix with a map?
   a) To see how far you have travelled
   b) As a check on the current satellite geometry
   c) To check that the position fix is correct

4. Why is getting used to a GPS in good weather a sensible idea?
   a) A GPS works best in good weather
   b) It can be difficult to operate a GPS in bad weather
   c) GPS reception is often not good in bad weather

5. If a GPS will happily navigate you straight over a cliff, what should you always do?
   a) Consult your map and contour
   b) Look at your GPS frequently
   c) Understand clearly what the GPS is telling you

6. A GPS is not a substitute for but a safety addition to:
   a) Knowing the route
   b) A map and compass
   c) Checking off the navigational features

The answers can be found on page 165.

Right: Using a GPS in winter conditions

CHECK YOUR LEARNING

TASK 1

Plan a GPS Route on Foot

Imagine you are planning a scenic group walk for an autumn holiday. You are the walk leader and responsible for the group's safety. Your task is to plan a route on a paper map of your choice. Then, if you have one, transfer that route to a compatible digital mapping system. You should consider GPS waypoint placement and time management in your route planning.

- Your walk should be about 10km in length.
- You should only use rights of way.
- Your party includes several children.
- The route should be within the capabilities of all.
- There should be a planned escape route.
- Your walk must be completed in daylight. The walk is planned for the end of October.
- Your party would like to finish the walk in a pub with a meal.

If you have a digital mapping system:
- transfer the route to your GPS;
- the route needs to saved to a folder on your PC;
- everyone has digital mapping and would like to receive an e-mailed copy of the route, which should include start time, meeting point, distance, total height gain, and total distance.

Left: A typical bike mount

TASK 2

Plan a GPS Route on a Mountain Bike

Your task is to plan a route for yourself and some friends for an expedition by bike in March and then, if you have a digital mapping system, to transfer that route to a compatible digital map. You should consider waypoint placement, upcoming turn information and time management in your route planning. Your ride should be a full day trip and end in daylight.

- Your mates would like to finish the ride at a country pub.
- The route should be within the capabilities of all.
- You must only use rights of way.
- There should be some challenging climbs and descents.
- Consider any safety implications for the ride.
- Do you need an escape route?

If you have a digital mapping system:
- the route needs to saved to a folder on your PC;
- everyone has digital mapping and would like to receive an e-mailed copy of the route, which should include start time, meeting point, distance, total height gain, and total distance.

Right: Comparing position fixes using Magellan eXplorist GPS

T A S K   3

If you have access to a digital mapping system, modify one of the routes created in Tasks 1 and 2.

- Imagine you have received the planned route from your leader.
  You wish to modify the route and make a few suggestions about it before the event.
- Save the route to a folder on your PC.
- Import the route into your mapping software.
- Review the profile of the route.
- Check the height and distance data.
- View the route in 3D and Fly Through if available to you.

You have decided that the route needs some amendments:
- add two waypoints to the route;
- drop one waypoint from the route;
- change the finishing destination;
- e-mail the amendments to the walk leader.

07

More Uses for your GPS

In a world of easy travel it is understandable that people who use GPS and digital mapping systems at home would wish to use them abroad. But that's not all you can do with your GPS: you can also download pre-coded routes and participate in GPS-based activities such as geocaching and geotrailing.

Using your GPS Abroad

A growing trend is for travellers to purchase a digital map for the country they intend to travel to and then plan their expeditions and pre-load routes and important waypoint information into their GPS systems ready for use whilst en route to and at their destination.

If you wish to use your GPS in another country or map format then your GPS setting must reflect the map you are using:

- The map position format must be the same as the map you are using. Look in the map legend.
- The map datum must be the same as the map you are using. Look in the map legend.
- The map units for distance and elevation should be the same as your map.
- The North reference should reflect the magnetic variation at your international location. This can be more than 20° in some parts of the world, so it is quite significant. You can find out what this is from the legend of your map.

Details of how to change these settings can be found in the *Step-by-Step Guide* on pages 67 to 95 and in the *Using your GPS Abroad* diagrams overleaf.

Many countries have their own map position formats, so the GPS manufacturers build in many international position formats and map data as part of the software. In the unlikely event that you are in a location that isn't covered by GPS international settings, you will need to enter the co-ordinates into what is called a 'user grid'. Getting your head around user grids is not for the non-technical so if you would like to know more, we have an explanatory paper available from GPS Training on request.

expert tip

Look for GPS friendly maps when you buy.
Many paper maps like IGN in France produce special GPS-friendly maps which make life a lot easier when route planning.

expert tip

When you have your GPS set up, check its operation by looking at the grid reference it gives you for a known current position abroad, such as your hotel, before you rely on it in wild country.

Left: Sir Chris Bonington uses his GPS to navigate on previously unclimbed peaks

USING YOUR GPS ABROAD

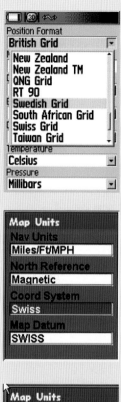

The best way to find out the information you need is to ask your map supplier. They should be able to ensure that the map you are using is GPS compatible. Be aware that some countries have a number of different mapping systems, only some of which might be GPS compatible.

It is worth noting that you can use different grid systems in the same country, for instance in the UK you can use British Grid or you could, if you prefer, use Latitude and Longitude. Our maps support both formats although the British Grid is much, much easier to use.

CHECK YOUR LEARNING

1. **In which countries in the world can you not use a GPS?**
   a) South of the 40th parallel
   b) There aren't any!
   c) Countries in which the USA has blocked satellite reception

2. **Who should you ask for the information you need to set your GPS up abroad?**
   a) The GPS manufacturer
   b) The British Embassy for the country you are going to visit
   c) Your map supplier

3. **Which one of the following is incorrect in relation to setting your GPS up for use abroad?**
   a) Select the correct position format
   b) Select the correct country
   c) Select the correct navigation units

The answers can be found on page 165.

TASK:

Imagine you are taking a trip to Zermatt, and wish to use your GPS in the resort:
• set your GPS to use Swiss Grid;
• reset your GPS for use in British Grid.

Using your GPS Abroad

 GARMIN.

Position references are just codes and mean nothing without the map to enable you to work out where the position is on the ground. Buy a 'GPS friendly' map that tells you the position format and map datum it uses. You will usually find this in the map legend area. Test your GPS abroad with its new settings by confirming the grid reference it gives you for a known position, such as your hotel, before you depend on it in wild country. **NOTE:** Depending on where you are you may also need to change the *North Reference*.

1

From the main menu page, select **Setup ❶** and then **Units**.

2

Highlight the **Position Format** window ❷ and press **Enter** to show the drop-down window containing the list of formats. Scroll up/down the list to find the position format for the map you are using (in this example – *Swedish*) and press the **Enter** button.

3

Note that the **Map Datum** window ❸ has changed automatically to the correct datum for the format we have entered. If this doesn't happen automatically on your GPS, you will have to change it manually to match your map.

4

If we now try to **Mark** a waypoint, we will see the location shown in the new Swedish Grid (SG) format ❹. As always, we can see details of the bearing to navigate ❺ and the distance to travel to Stockholm ❻. Remember to change back to *British Grid* on your return to the UK.

MAGELLAN®

Position references are just codes and mean nothing without the map to enable you to work out where the position is on the ground. Buy a 'GPS friendly' map that tells you the position format and map datum it uses. You will usually find this in the map legend area. Test your GPS abroad with its new settings by confirming the grid reference it gives you for a known position, such as your hotel, before you depend on it in wild country. **NOTE:** Depending on where you are you may also need to change the *North Reference*.

1

Press the **Menu** button, highlight **Preferences** and press the **Enter** button. Now highlight *Map Units* ❶ and press **Enter** again.

2

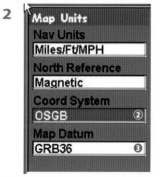

Highlight the **Coord System** window ❷ (currently set to OSGB) and press the **Enter** button to show the list.

Depending on where you are you may also need to change the **North Reference** ❸ too.

3

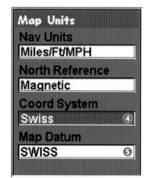

Choose the **Co-ordinate System** you need (in this example – *Swiss* grid) ❹ and press the **Enter** button. Normally the **Map Datum** ❺ will change automatically. If this does not happen, change it manually.

4

All points of interest will now be shown in the coding of the new **Coord System**, Swiss Grid in this example. ❻ Remember to change back to *OSGB* on your return to the UK.

Making GPS Fun

Initially GPSs were thought of as 'toys for boys'. Now however the technology has universal appeal, as male and female, young and old alike explore its capabilities. This has lead to the creation of ways to apply GPS technology in the outdoors which are both educational and interesting.

In previous chapters we explored the safety aspects of GPS. In this chapter we will look at ways in which GPS and mapping systems can give you the means to journey to places you may not have considered before.

The combination of GPS and mapping systems can open new horizons for the traveller and recreation user. You could now:

- pre-plan routes and journeys in the comfort of your home;
- buy digital mapping software from around the world;
- prepare routes at home and download into a GPS;
- download ready prepared routes from the Internet (pre-coded routes);
- purchase CD ROMs with ready prepared walks and scrambles;
- join the growing band of worldwide geocachers;
- record previously travelled routes and tracks into a file on your PC;
- explore ways to use these systems to record information and locations associated with your hobbies and interests.

Ready Prepared GPS Routes
One of the joys of owning a mapping system is to be able to sit down on a cold winter's evening and plan routes for the future. Although the study of maps can be both interesting and rewarding, planning journeys in unfamiliar areas is daunting for most of us. But don't worry – help is at hand.

Precoded routes for walking, scrambling or biking are routes ready-made for downloading to a GPS. These come as either a package of trails on a CD ROM or as a download from the Internet. Downloading routes from the Internet offers the traveller the most flexibility and variety. Access to Internet routes is usually through an annual subscription or in return for a payment for each route downloaded.

One of the leading sites is www.walkingworld.com. Here over 170 local contributors share their favourite routes with you with nearly 3,000 to choose from. Walks are available throughout the British Isles and they have recently introduced walks in both France and Spain. Every UK walk comes with an easy-to-follow photographic guide, a section of Ordnance Survey mapping, or a *Memory-Map* route file with GPS co-ordinates.

Right: Walkingworld homepage on the Internet

Right: Go4awalk homepage on the Internet

We also recommend visiting www.Go4awalk.com where you will find downloadable route maps and GPS waymarks for all UK walks, footpaths, trails and much more. Both sites have useful accommodation guides.

Geocaching and Geotrailing

This is a fun area for GPS users, growing in popularity amongst young and old alike, with a massive following worldwide. At our last count there were over 700,000 websites worldwide. The sport has a detailed set of rules and etiquette. The accepted regulators of the sport are www.geocaching.com. Visit this site for more information. You will be amazed at the variety of fun opportunities on offer for you to become involved with.

Kids love Geocaching. It turns a dull boring walk with Mum and Dad into a treasure hunt with a reward at the end. What child can resist that?

What is Geocaching?

In its most basic form geocaching is a treasure hunt for a 'cache' or hidden treasure. To take part, you receive a clue and/or a grid reference or position and use your GPS to reach the cache. A cache should only be located following the Geocaching code. More information and guidance on the rules and etiquette can be found on the Geocaching.com website.

Virtual Caches

Here you get a position reference and a question for the player to answer to prove that the cache has been found. A virtual cache could be almost anything you care to think of, such as a name on the gate or similar. The beauty of a virtual cache is that it is usually there for a long time.

Geotrails (Multi-Caches)

To follow a geotrail you receive a position and clue to your first cache, in which you will find a position and clue to your next cache and so on until you reach the end of the trail.

More about Geotrailing

We use caches and virtual caches on our training courses. They are an excellent way of getting practical experience of newly acquired GPS skills. We put together some multi-caches of our own for training purposes and our students found them interesting, challenging and a good test of their navigation skills.

One of our course venues is a superb old coaching inn. With the support of the landlord we laid out a trail based on the principle of multi-caching. In the penultimate cache there was a password and players who took the password to the final cache (behind the bar) received a pint as a reward for completing the challenge. Geotrailing was born!

Right Geocaching.com homepage on the Internet
Below: Geocacher reaching the cache

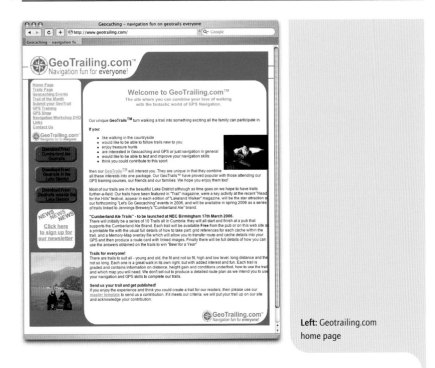

Left: Geotrailing.com home page

We have since established our own website www.geotrailing.com where you will find a series of virtual trails to test your GPS skills, available as free downloads. If you enjoy our trails, you can send us your own trail and have it published on the Web. We also create a Geotrail challenge for each edition of a national walking magazine, that usually ends with a free drink at a local pub.

T A S K

Create a Geotrail

You have some young relations coming to stay and are looking for a way to keep them entertained for a day. Your task is to create a treasure trail for them to follow.

Follow these easy instructions to create your own Geotrail:

Before you leave home:
- plan the walk you have in mind, think about where you would place waypoints and try and include something interesting in the walk, such as a castle or boat trip;
- make sure you take with you a map, GPS and a notebook to record cache information;
- clear your track log and trip computer before you start.

On the trail, record the following information:
- mark your position at start of the trail;
- as you proceed look out for suitable places that will make a virtual cache (a location where you can ask the player to answer a question about that location to prove they are in the correct place);
- when you have decided on your virtual cache, mark your position in your GPS and record the information into your notebook along with the cache clue;
- try to locate about ten caches for each trail and place the caches at significant turning places.

On your return:
- if you have a mapping system, download your track and marks into your mapping system;
- use the position co-ordinates/clues to create your virtual geotrail.

You could prepare an interesting list/trail sheet for your players which should contain for each virtual cache, a grid reference and clue (you could even include a photo of your cache if you wished to be really clever) and a space to write in the answers.

Think about a reward for successful completion of your trail – sweeties are good.

If you complete this task, not only will you have some fun but you will be testing your GPS skills such as: creating waypoints on the hoof, route planning with GPS in mind, the transfer of data between GPS and mapping system (if you have one), and the ability to review a track log and change it to a route ready for use in a trail in the future.

Additional Partners for your GPS and Digital Maps

PDAs and Pocket PCs

PDA stands for **Personal Digital Assistant** and is an all-encompassing name for all handheld devices and covers Palm, Pocket PC, and Smartphones (a PDA and phone combined in one unit). Pocket PCs use *Microsoft® Windows® Mobile* as the operating system. Other types of PDA tend to use different operating systems. From now on we shall refer to them all as PDAs.

Left: Using a PDA in the field

PDAs are a growing sector of the market place. The main attraction is that by combining a PDA and GPS and then exploiting links to a PC you can achieve the ultimate combination – your actual position shown on high quality digital topographic mapping (such as the OS 1:25,000) displayed on a high resolution screen updated in real time as you move.

It is possible to link a PDA to a GPS and then use both whilst on the move. As PDAs are very small computers, most can be loaded with a digital mapping system. When the GPS is operating, the cross-haired circle in the middle of the screen marks your location on the map. The screen picture automatically adjusts every second to show your new location as you move.

e x p e r t   t i p

When purchasing a PDA consider those with the ability to accept a memory card. Most will. Memory cards will allow you to download much larger segments of mapping (dependent on the PDA model you have) but will also give you the flexibility to use different memory cards for the mapping of different areas or countries.

Most mapping software will have the ability to transfer data to a PDA which, when combined with a software package provided by a compatible PDA unit, will allow the user to import segments of digital mapping into the PDA. The limiting factor to the amount of mapping you can download to a PDA is the memory available. Nearly all Pocket PCs will work with a digital mapping system but some other types of PDA are not yet compatible with some mapping systems, so always check before buying.

As with so many types of technology, this is a fast-moving market. The parameters of what might be possible are changing, which in its turn is fuelling the imagination of users and writers of software applications. The great advantage of this type of product is it takes the PDA into the outdoors, opening the door to many great software solutions. The disadvantage, as far as most walkers and bikers are concerned, is its fragility and the difficulty of making it water-proof. All these issues can be addressed in various ways, but we feel someone on a mountain bike might not wish to have £400 worth of PDA kit on their handlebars when they hit the deck!

We believe therefore that this type of hardware solution will appeal more to the user who wishes to combine recreational use with in-car navigation. As an additional bonus they will still have all the other features contained in a PDA such as word processing, e-mail and so on. This will remain a dynamic market and those wishing to buy into this technology should make sure they do some homework in terms of what's on the market before taking the plunge.

GPS links

There are several ways to link the unit to a GPS receiver:

By Cable:

This is simply a cable link between a PDA and a GPS with a cable connector. The downside of this solution is you carry two pieces of kit. The cables must have the correct connectors at each end, and can be quite expensive.

Wireless (Bluetooth)

This usually uses a GPS that has no screen and is called a GPS egg or puck. This sits in or on your rucksack and will transmit short-range signals to your PDA, which will process the information and display it on screen.

GPS Sleeve

The PC slots into a GPS receiver (a NAVMAN sleeve is a popular version) and connects the two. This is a neat way of solving the problem of dual pieces of kit.

Integrated PC and GPS

This is a natural progression of the GPS sleeve – build the two into one box. The advantage is that you retain the looks of the PDA and have smaller, neater unit. In most cases you just flip up the antenna when required.

Integrated Phone and GPS

Integrated mobile and GPS are just starting to emerge onto the market. These have great potential. Where this development will lead is unclear, although we consider the future of GPS in the final chapter. A GPS phone would suit the user who wishes to access map related information and directions whilst on the move.

Where and what to buy?

The best advice we can give you is to firstly decide on the mapping software you wish to purchase, then look at what hardware is compatible or recommended for use with that software and finally make sure both are compatible with your PC.

Most of the software houses provide links on their website to providers of compatible hardware. Armed with this information, shop around both on the high street and the Internet.

Navman

Probably the leading manufacturer of satellite navigation systems that specialise in this market is Navman, The brand was established in New Zealand in 1988 and is part of the international Brunswick Corporation. They provide high quality innovative products, sales and support in a very technical market. In 2004 they launched the **Navman Pin**, one of the first integrated PC/GPS.

Website: www.navman.co.uk for both sales and technical support.

Below: A NavMan PIN

CHECK YOUR LEARNING

1. What is a PDA?
   a) A pocket PC that uses the Navman operating system
   b) A pocket PC that may not be Microsoft® compatible
   c) A pocket PC that uses Microsoft® operating system

2. If you had a GPS puck/egg how would it communicate with your PDA?
   a) By cable
   b) By short range signals
   c) By satellite signals

3. What should you ensure before buying any PC/PDA?
   a) It is GPS compatible
   b) It is compatible with your digital mapping system
   c) It is compatible with the Ordnance Survey system

The answers can be found on page 165.

ADDITIONAL PARTNERS FOR YOUR GPS AND DIGITAL MAPS

Auto Navigation Software

This has the potential to be a huge growth area, as users of handheld units seek to combine using GPS not only outdoors, but also in the car. Before we look at this growing market trend, let's consider what other forms of in-car navigation systems are on the market.

Below: A Garmin GPSmap 60CS on an auto navigation mount
Bottom: A NavMan PIN with an in-car mount

There are three ways to access the software:

- dedicated in-car Sat-Nav systems;
- combining a PDA/Integrated GPS and auto navigation software;
- linking a handheld colour mapping GPS with auto navigation software.

In-car Systems

These days many top-of-the-range cars come with auto navigation as standard. The level of sophistication offered will vary but will mainly depend on memory size. Some in-car systems come with up to 1Gb memory and navigation software that encompasses a whole continent. A typical system will offer the following:

- street maps with points of interest;
- automatic route calculation and recalculation;
- turn-by-turn voice guidance;
- transfer of information by cable to/from PC;
- powered via 12V adaptor cable;
- track log and trip computer;
- track log should allow you to retrace your path;
- in-car mount if the system is not built in.

PDA/Integrated GPS and Auto Navigation Software

As technology moves on, more flexible options become available to combine both in-car navigation and outdoor navigation. One fairly new innovation is to combine both PDA and GPS in a small compact unit, and then sell it as a bundle with a auto navigation software package, in-car mount, and power and data transfer cables.

The advantage of this type of combination is its flexibility, and if you ensure that the hardware you purchase is compatible with one of the major digital mapping software packages, you will have the advantage of being able to download OS maps. With this option you still retain the ability to have turn-by-turn voice guidance.

The downside could be that this type of product is not waterproof or very robust.

Handheld Colour Mapping GPS and Auto Navigation Software

With this sort of combination you can set off from home navigating a route to the top of the hill you wish to go to today. The system will give you turn-by-turn navigation to get you to the start of the walk and then continue navigating you off road to get you to the summit.

The key to this development has been the introduction of colour screens for the handheld GPS and the availability of purpose-developed auto navigation software. Now the outdoor user can purchase a unit that has the capability (with extra purchased software) to cover on and off road usage.

Possible shortcomings of using a handheld GPS in the car could be the size of screen and the current lack of voice turn guidance. Turn prompts will be by way of a beep alarm that is quite adequate but not quite as specific or reassuring as a voice. Other than that, the combined system should give you all the important features of a standard in-car system.

How the GPS provides memory for the software could be key to you deciding which model to purchase. GPS have two ways to provide memory, either as fixed memory (usually up to 115Mb) or by the use of Secure Digital (SD) cards.

At present SD cards give the user the option of downloading larger chunks of software to the GPS unit, plus the ability to perhaps have auto software on one card and topo mapping or marine software on another.

One key advantage here is that handheld GPS are designed for use on the hill and are robust and waterproof!

What Does the Future Hold for GPS?

Although the concept of GPS was invented in 1960, it was 1989 before the first commercial handheld GPS device was launched to the USA market by Magellan. Since then development in GPS technology has been continually accelerating.

It is always difficult to predict the future for any technology but we can learn much from the way the computer, and to some extent the mobile phone, has developed. Some of the relevant trends that applied to these technologies were:

- smaller devices;
- cheaper devices;
- more memory;
- better quality screens and transition from black and white to colour;
- the use of images (icons) to replace 'wordy' commands;
- more user-friendliness with intuitive responses;
- improved robustness and reliability;
- data storage devices with much more capacity and faster access to stored data;
- more powerful batteries with faster recharging;
- portability;
- introduction of sound;
- convergence, or combining of functions into one device.

In recent years we have seen GPS become smaller and significantly cheaper – early GPS weighed nearly 1lb! At the same time, typical GPS memory has increased from 100 waypoints and 1 route to 1000 waypoints and 50 routes – and virtually unlimited on some models. Screen quality has progressed from very low-resolution mono colour LCDs to 256 colour TFT displays. Some displays will now convert to 'night-time colours' at sunset automatically.

Early GPS relied on the user knowing what to do with a cryptic display on the screen. These days images or icons on the screen suggest what a button does and commands, that can be shown in a number of major languages, are presented in relatively easy-to-understand menus. In many cases the GPS operating system will highlight the command it thinks you need at a particular stage in a process to make life easier.

Another aspect of user-friendliness is the ability of many GPS to display certain types of proprietary maps on the screen to orientate the user to their surroundings. This was impossible until memory became both very small and very cheap. For example, today's top of the range GPS can hold street level mapping for the whole of the UK in its memory with space to spare. This has been improved still further by using removable secure digital storage cards that can hold mapping and routes for particular areas or even for whole countries. These devices can provide an endless source of storage.

GPS, like computers, have become more robust and reliable, and will stay waterproof even when dropped into up to a metre of water for up to 30 minutes. Modern GPS can now track up to 14 satellites and with WAAS/EGNOS have become five times more accurate than earlier devices.

Without charged batteries, GPS are useless. In the early days GPS used three or four batteries that lasted only up to four hours. Today's models will give up to 30 hours use, some with lithium batteries that can be recharged in around an hour or less.

In terms of portability, GPS are small and light enough to be put in a pocket and can be set up to operate with the map formats and datum of virtually any country across the world with easy adjustment to magnetic variation for any location world-wide.

Today we use computers and mobile phones for many additional functions like music and films as well as to listen to the radio and get voice instructions on how to do something. Although PDAs and sat-nav systems will give voice prompting, handheld GPS have yet to harness this technology.

Lastly is the overarching trend of convergence where different functions that were originally separate are combined into one device. This has been a past and current force of some significance on the development of computers and mobile phones and, we believe, GPS will be no exception in the future.

Our best 'guesstimate' is that the future for GPS is likely to be characterised by:

Within around 5 years:
- The widespread use of both removable memory cards with high storage capacity and rechargeable Li-ion batteries
- High-resolution colour screens becoming standard
- Increasing use of extended Points of Information databases to find services, entertainment, emergency services, food, accommodation, shopping and attractions with a GPS.
- Convergence between the functions of handheld GPS, sat-nav, portable computer and mobile phone into one small portable unit. This would be the ultimate navigational and communication device capable of being used with optimal efficiency either on or off road, in town and in country. It would be rugged and waterproof with the capability of showing a tile of topographical map, such as Ordnance Survey, or street map on the screen as well being capable of word processing and so on, Internet, e-mails, texts and mobile phone. For now, let's call these converged navigation devices (CNDs).

- GPS hardware will continue to fall in price even though power and functionality will increase.
- Digital mapping companies will start to diversify into the provision of value added map related information services.

Within around 10 years:
- Voice command prompts accepted by a CND from the user and a voice help function possibly linked by Bluetooth to an earphone.
- Automated setup of functions like which tile of map to display and magnetic variation according to actual location.
- Accuracy improved still further with the introduction of Galileo – Europe's own dedicated satellite system.
- Increasing use of CNDs by the public as the means both to find location-based information and to be navigated there.
- Simple GPS devices being sold in supermarkets and garages as a virtual commodity.
- New markets being developed in software based information services to be bought or rented via the Internet to be used on CNDs.
- GPS hardware with more functionality will continue to fall in price whilst the cost of GPS based information services is likely to increase with demand for such services.

In the more distant future:
- The rental of tiles of mapping downloaded from the internet straight into a CND. This would be ideal for holidays abroad.
- We could see the GPS screen projected holographically into the goggles or sunglasses of the user, possibly even into the air in front of them.
- CNDs and GPS based information services diffused across the developed world and accepted as a normal tool for living.

Whatever the future for GPS may hold, there is little doubt that the technology will move at an ever-increasing rate into our mainstream lives. However the basic functionality of today's handheld GPS will remain. For this reason, we believe that the investment you make today in learning how to use a GPS safely and effectively will undoubtedly equip you well for the foreseeable future and beyond.

Appendices

GLOSSARY

2D reception	A GPS position fix from just the two co-ordinates – latitude and longitude. It is not as accurate as a *3D fix* and requires at least three 'visible' satellites.
3D reception	A GPS position fix from three co-ordinates – latitude, longitude and elevation. It requires at least four 'visible' satellites and is more accurate than a *2D fix*.
Accuracy	A measure of how close a given GPS position is to the true position. For example, an accuracy of 10m puts you somewhere within a circle on the ground with a 20m diameter.
Activate	To start to navigate a route.
Active Leg	That part of the route currently being navigated.
Altimeter	A device for measuring altitude based on barometric pressure.
Altitude	The current elevation described in feet or metres above sea level as calculated by the GPS barometer. *(See Elevation).*
Averaging	A process used by some GPS to average position fixes whilst stationary in order to give a more precise final fix reading.
Backtrack	A route created from a saved track that can be navigated in reverse to get back to the starting point.
Basemap	A basic map built into mapping GPS. It will usually show villages, towns, cities, main roads, railways, rivers and lakes.
Bearing	The compass direction from the current location to the next *waypoint*.
BRG	Abbreviation for *bearing*.

Contour (to)	To proceed over the flattest ground possible by following the contour line of the terrain.
Co-ordinate system	The grid format chosen by the user to show the position fix on the GPS map screen. In the UK this would be the *Ordnance Survey National Grid*, abbreviated to OSGB or BNG
Co-ordinates	A unique set of numbers (and often letters) that describe a position on a map.
Datum	*See Map Datum.*
Default	A setting automatically chosen by the GPS unless changed by the user.
Distance	The distance between the current position and the next waypoint or landmark. This is usually measured by GPS as an 'over-the earth' distance rather than a straight line.
DST	Abbreviation for *distance*.
EGNOS	**European Geostationary Navigational Overlay Service** – the European equivalent of the American WAAS system. EGNOS is fully compatible with WAAS (*See WAAS*).
Elevation	Current elevation described in feet or metres above sea level as calculated by the GPS satellite system. *(See altitude).*
EPE	Estimated position error. For example, an EPE of 10m puts you somewhere within a circle on the ground with a 20m diameter.
ETA	Abbreviation for the estimated time that you should arrive at the destination based on current speed.
Final distance	The distance between current position and final destination. This is usually measured by GPS as an 'over-the earth' distance rather than a straight line.

Galileo	The EU's GPS satellite system currently under development. When this is fully implemented, the EU will not be reliant on the USA GPS system.
Geocaching	A form of treasure hunt using a GPS to navigate to given *co-ordinates*.
Geotrailing	A form of *geocache* developed by **GPSTraining** that involves multiple caches where the 'treasure' is the co-ordinates for the next cache.
GLONASS	The Russian equivalent of the American WAAS system. GLONASS is fully compatible with WAAS (*see WAAS*).
GoTo	A simple straight-line route from current location to one destination waypoint.
Grid North	North direction as given by the vertical grid lines on a map.
Grid reference	A *co-ordinate* calculated by reference to a grid system such as the Ordnance Survey National Grid. A grid system is a set of equally spaced horizontal and vertical lines overlaid onto a map to form a series of square areas or grids.
Heading	Actual direction of travel with reference to north
HDG	Abbreviation for *heading*.
Initialisation	The process of setting up the GPS including making it aware of its current location. After initialisation, the GPS remembers its location and acquires a position fix more quickly as it knows which satellites to look for.
Landmarks	Locations that have been stored in the GPS for later use. (*See also Waypoint and Points of Interest*)
LAT/LON	Abbreviation for latitude and longitude.
LMK	Abbreviation for landmark or waypoint.
Magnetic North	North direction as given by a magnetic compass.

Magnetic variation	The difference in degrees between magnetic north and true north. In much of the UK, this is currently about 4° west.
Map Datum	The model that a mapmaker uses to convert the spherical shape of the globe into a two dimensional map. This can usually be found in the legend of the map. In the UK, we use OSGB or GRB36.
Mark	To register the co-ordinates of the current position for editing and/or saving in the GPS for future use.
Naismith's Rule	A rule of thumb to calculate the time it would take to walk a particular route. It was created by the Scottish mountaineer WW Naismith in 1892. The basis of the rule is to assume speed over flat ground at 3mph (12 minutes to 1km) and then add 1 minute for each 10m contour line (on 1:25,000 Explorer maps) ascended and ½ minute for each 10m contour line descended. The settings button within many digital mapping software products allows the components of Naismith's rule to be tailored to your personal preferences.
North up orientation	This fixes the GPS map or plot display so that north is always 'up' or towards the top edge of the screen.
Odometer	A device that measures overall distance travelled since it was last reset.
Points of Interest (POI)	Locations that have been stored in the GPS for later use. These may include locations of different types, such as garages, hospitals, restaurants and so on, downloaded from proprietory software.
PDA	Abbreviation for Personal Digital Assistant. A term that includes Pocket PCs and other types of PDA.
Position fix	The co-ordinates that establish the current position.
Position format	The grid format chosen by the user to show the position fix on the GPS map screen. In the UK this would be the Ordnance Survey National Grid. This is often abbreviated to BNG or OSGB.

Reverse	To reverse the order of a route or backtrack. For example, from 'begin' to 'end' to 'end' to 'begin'.
Romer	A scaling device that can be overlaid on a map to make grid reference calculation easier and more accurate.
Route	A name for a number of waypoints or landmarks grouped together in the order in which they are to be navigated.
SPD	Abbreviation for speed.
Statute	Refers to the use of miles and feet as a unit of measure.
Topographic map	A map that shows contour lines to represent height above sea level as well as other features.
Tracback	A route created from a saved track that can be navigated to get back to the starting point.
Track	A record in the GPS of movements across the ground whilst travelling on a specific journey.
Track History	*See Track Log*.
Track up orientation	This fixes the GPS map or plot display so that the direction of travel is always 'up' or towards the top edge of the screen.
Track log	A record in the GPS of movements across the ground in all the journeys made since the track log was last reset.
Trackroute	A route created from the track of the current route that can then itself be navigated.
TRK	Abbreviation for *track*.
TRN	Abbreviation for *turn*.
True North	The direction to the North Pole from the current position.

TTG	Abbreviation for time to go (until the destination will be reached).
Turn	The change needed to the current heading to get back on course to the next waypoint.
User landmarks	Landmarks created by the user in contrast to those already stored in the GPS automatically, such as cities.
WAAS	Abbreviation for Wide Area Augmentation System. This system uses extra geostationary satellites linked to ground stations to provide a more accurate position fix (usually up to 5 times more accurate). The system can only be used by GPS that are WAAS-enabled.
Waypoints	Locations that have been stored in the GPS for later use. Also known as *landmarks* and *points of interest (POI)*.

Answers to "Check your Learning" Questions

Page 7 – 1: b, 2: a, 3: c, 4: b, 5: b, 6: b

Page 15 – 1: b, 2: c, 3: b, 4: c, 5: c

Page 55 – 1: b, 2: c, 3: a, 4: c

Page 127 – 1: c, 2: b, 3: a, 4: c, 5: b, 6: a

Page 134 – 1: a, 2: c, 3: c, 4: b, 5: a, 6: b

Page 141 – 1: b, 2: c, 3: b

Page 153 – 1: b, 2: b, 3: b

25 Questions

to ask yourself before you complete the
User GPS Checklist on page169. Check our
general recommendations on page 168 first.

Some questions for you to ponder	Some notes from GPSTraining	Your own notes
How am I going to use a GPS?	Your uses now and in the future?	
Am I just going to use it to confirm my position?	A GPS will do a lot more than just this.	
How complex a GPS do I want?	Some sophisticated GPS are relatively easy to use.	
Should I just buy something simple?	Be sure that this type of GPS is all you will ever need.	
Do I need an electronic compass?	Gives an instant bearing even when stationary.	
Do I need an electronic altimeter?	Useful if you are at altitude (above 3,000m) and/or want pressure trends to forecast weather changes.	
Will I want to create waypoints, routes and tracks?	Most users find they do, but not perhaps initially.	
How many waypoints, routes and tracks do I need?	Unless you are a long distance walker, average numbers of these should be enough.	
Will I want to exchange this data with my PC?	You probably will, but perhaps later.	
Am I interested in downloading waypoints and routes?	You will, unless you want to enter them manually which is very tedious.	
Should I use a mapping system to do this?	A mapping system is probably the easiest way of getting data into your GPS.	
Do I need a serial or a USB connection?	Check your computer against the diagrams on pp109–110. A serial port is 9 pin D-shaped.	

Some questions for you to ponder	Some notes from GPSTraining	Your own notes
Am I interested in street mapping?	You can use your GPS to navigate by road with this.	
If so, will I have to download improved mapping into my GPS?	**Mapsource** (Garmin) or **Mapsend** (Magellan) are the products you will need to buy. A mapping GPS is needed.	
How much memory will I need to do this?	The more the better.	
Will maps and charts look better in colour?	Most certainly yes. How good is your computer screen?	
Do I need a colour screen on my GPS?	The maps will look so much clearer with a colour screen.	
How good is my eyesight? Do I need a larger screen?	If you need glasses, you should get the biggest screen.	
Should I combine a GPS with a PDA?	Bigger screen and many uses but not very robust.	
Would I have other uses for a PDA?	It is a fully functional pocket PC, but is not waterproof without a special cover.	
Do I want to see Ordnance Survey mapping on my PDA?	You can see a purchased OS map image on this with your current position overlaid on it as you move.	
Will I use Memory-Map to do this?	We believe it is the best product on the market.	
How much do I wish to spend?	Cables and maps are extras – budget them in.	
If I buy a basic model, have I allowed for future use?	Spend a little more now and save in the long term?	
Would I find a GPSTraining course helpful?	This will give you hands-on experience and expert advice before you buy and should prove a wise investment.	

GPS Checklist

We have completed this checklist with our general recommendations to help you. You can use the blank checklist that follows to create your own GPS profile then take this with you when you compare different products.

Features	Essential[1]	Desirable[2]
WAAS enabled	✓	
Database for at least 500 waypoints	✓	
Capacity to store at least 20 routes and 10 tracks	✓	
Exchange data between the GPS and PC	✓	
Good quality colour screen		✓
Database of points of interest		✓
Memory to store extra points of interest and street mapping (probably essential for bikers)	✓	✓
Electronic compass & barometric altimeter		✓
Elevation profile on screen		✓
Audible proximity alarm		✓
User friendly buttons and menus (Try before you buy)	✓	
Fits comfortably in the palm of your hand	✓	
Waterproof to IPX7 standard	✓	
Cable, case & lanyard included		✓
USB cable included or available at a reasonable price	✓	
Downloadable firmware upgrades		✓
Have you thought of the future? **Will you need the desirable things later?**	✓	

1. I will not buy a GPS without these features

2. These features are nice to have if the price is right but are not essential

User GPS Checklist

Use this checklist to build your ideal GPS systems profile, then use it to find the best deal. Do make sure that you compare like with like. Some retailers bundle maps with GPS as a package. They may or may not be a good deal.

My ideal GPS profile
Budget: Minimum £ _____ Maximum £ _____

Features	Essential[1]	Desirable[2]	Not Needed[3]
WAAS enabled			
Database for at least 500 waypoints			
Capacity to store at least 20 routes and 10 tracks			
Exchange data between GPS and PC			
Good quality colour screen			
Base map with towns and cities included			
Memory capacity to store extra points of interest and street mapping			
Electronic compass			
Electronic altimeter			
Elevation profile on screen			
Audible proximity alarm			
User friendly buttons and menus (Try before you buy)			
Fits comfortably in the palm of my hand			
Waterproof to IPX7 standard			
Cable, case & lanyard included			
Downloadable software upgrades			
Thinking of the future, will you need the desirable features later?			
Other features you might want to consider:			
Large screen & large images on it (important if you wear glasses)			
Size of GPS			
Weight of GPS			
Geocaching features			
External antennae interface (useful if using in a car in cities)			
Other features:			

1. I will not buy a GPS without these features
2. These features are nice to have if the price is right but are not essential
3. I will not pay extra for these features as I will never use them

Index

2D fix 13, 37
3D fix 13, 14, 37, 62, 64

A

accuracy 12, 18, 37, 63, 122, 123, 124
Anquet Technology 106
antennae 14
augmentation signals – *see Satellite Based Augmentation Systems*

B

BackTrack 65, 94, 129, 131
barometric altimeter 41
    calibration of 47
basemaps 24
batteries 46, 47, 128
bearing 5
breadcrumb trail 64, 65
British Grid 4, 42, 60, 70

C

click stick – *see keys/buttons*
compass 2
    bearing 5
    heading 5
    Romer scale 5
    use of a ~ 5

D

digital mapping 22, 59, 63
digital mapping software 16, 17

E

EGNOS – *see Satellite Based Augmentation Systems*

electronic compass 38
    calibration of 38, 46
ENTER key – *see keys/buttons*
escape route 16, 124, 131
European Geostationary Navigation Overlay Service (EGNOS) – *see Satellite Based Augmentation Systems*

F

factory settings 34
    navigational data 54
false signals – *see reception*
features – *see GPS functions*
FIND key – *see keys/buttons*
frequently asked questions (FAQs) 28
Fugawi 107
future-proofing 25

G

GARMIN GPS
For a list of diagrams illustrating setup and functions, see *Index of Diagrams* on page 176

Garmin xi, 16, 17, 19, 26, 30, 36, 59, 68, 154
    eTrex GPS xi, 68
geocaching 146
    virtual caches 146
geotrailing 29, 146
    multi-caches 146
global positioning satellite system – *see GPS Systems*
GOTO key – *see keys/buttons*
GoTo route 59, 60, 129
    create a ~ 87

GPS FUNCTIONS
For a list of diagrams illustrating GPS functions, see *Index of Diagrams* on pages 176–177

GPS functions 59
  averaging 59
  GoTo 62, 70, 72, 122, 131
  Help 86
  Mark 59, 60, 70, 84, 131, 142
  Route 63, 73, 74, 75, 77, 78, 88, 89, 92, 122
    getting the best out of the ~ function 124
  Track 64, 79, 80, 81
GPS systems 10
  accuracy of ~ – *see accuracy*
  choice of ~ 16
    buying on the high street 25
    buying online 24
    component 18
    entry level 18, 21
    future-proofing 25
    mapping 18, 21
  detail 21
  how they work 11
  mapping GPS 21, 155
  memory 21
  screen 21, 22, 155
  Secure Digital (SD) card 82, 155
  websites and support services 26
GPS Training 6, 25, 29, 30, 31, 140
  training courses 29, 30
GPS/PC connection – *see PC*
grid reference 5, 16, 60, 115, 118
grid systems 3
  British Grid – *see British Grid*
  latitude/longitude 3, 141
  user grid 140

H
hazards 60
heading 5
Health and Safety xii
  batteries 128
  position fix 129
  preparation 128, 129
  staying safe 131

I
in-car navigation 151, 154
IN/OUT key(s) – *see keys/buttons*
information sources 29
  DVD 30
  magazines 29
  user forums 28
  video 30
  websites 26
information windows 48
  changing views 48, 52
ionospheric error – *see reception*

K
keys/buttons 34
  arrow joystick 35
  Backlight 35
  Compass 35
  ENTER 34, 35
  Esc 35
  FIND 34, 35
  GOTO 34, 35
  IN/OUT 34
  MARK 34, 35
  MENU 34, 35
  Nav 35
  On/Off 35
  options 35
  PAGE 34, 35
  Power 35

QUIT 34, 35
SCROLL 34
thumb stick 35
zoom 35

L

landmarks – *see waypoints*
laptop – *see PC*
latitude/longitude 3
Lowrance 28

M

MAGELLAN GPS
For a list of diagrams illustrating
setup and functions, see *Index of*
***Diagrams* on page 177**

Magellan xi, 16, 17, 19, 26, 30, 36, 59,
64, 68
eXplorist GPS xi, 68
file storage system 82
map scale 39
mapping GPS – *see GPS systems*
maps 2
digital maps 3, 98
3D view 98
aviation charts 102
elevation 118
features 99
fly through 98
land-based 100
map units 50, 118, 140
marine charts 102
street maps 101, 154
types available 100
worldwide 103
OS maps 3
Explorer 3, 118
Landranger 3, 118

paper maps 3
route planning with ~ 114, 115
MARK key 34
Memory-Map 22, 30, 64, 65, 98, 102, 106
MENU key – *see keys/buttons*
menus 34
FIND 57
GOTO 58
main menu 34, 36
MENU 58
ROUTES 57
sub-menus 34
TRACKS 57
MSAS – *see Satellite Based*
Augmentation Systems
multipath error – *see reception*

N

Naismith's Rule 99, 125
navigation 2
traditional 2, 6
Navigation Workshop DVD 30
navigational data 54
factory input 54
how to find saved ~ 55
planned data 54
user database 60
user-created 54
navigation software – *see software*
Navman 19, 152, 154
North pointer 39

P

PAGE key – *see keys/buttons*
pages/screens 36
Barometer/Altimeter Page 41
Compass Page 38
stop navigating a route
from the ~ 76
Find Page 55

Highway Page 40
    stop navigating a route
        from the ~ 76
Main Menu 36
Map Page 39
    setup 45, 51
    stop navigating a route
        from the ~ 76
Position Page 41
Satellite Page 37
Trip Computer Page 40
patch aerial 14, 131
PC 17, 98
    connecting to ~ 108–109
        RS232/USB converter cable 110
        Serial Port 110
        USB Cable 111
    RS232 serial port 109
    RS232/USB converter cable 20, 109,
        110
    USB cable 20, 109, 110
PDA 17, 18, 150, 151
    ~ link to GPS 151
        cable 151
        GPS Sleeve 152
        wireless (Bluetooth) 151
    choosing a ~ 152
    combination PDA/GPS 150, 152, 154
    integrated Phone/GPS 152
personalising your GPS – see setup
points of interest – see waypoints
power up 34
pre-coded walks 29

Q

quadrifilar helix aerial 14, 131
QUIT key – see keys/buttons

R

reception 13
    false signal 13
    ionospheric error 14, 18
    multipath error 14, 18
reversed route – see route
Romer scale 5
route 16, 116
    ~ planning 114, 123, 124, 144
        ~ with a digital mapping system
            118
            compass bearing 118
            distances 118
            hill profiles 118
            journey length 118
            journey time 118
            terrain visualisation 118
        ~ with digital mapping system
            and GPS 121
            download tracks 121
            upload waypoints 121
        ~ with paper maps 114, 115
        be prepared 128
        tight horseshoe 124
        tips 124
    active route 75, 76
    amend a ~ 74, 89
    change order of waypoints 74
    change/replace a waypoint 74
    create a ~ 63, 73, 88
        Select Next Point 73
    Create Route screen 88
    Deactivate Route 91
    default route file 88, 90, 91, 92
    delete a ~ 78, 93
    insert a waypoint 74
    leg 116, 118
    name 73

navigate a ~ 16, 63, 73, 75, 90, 117
  stop navigating a ~ 75, 76, 91
    from the Active Route page 76
    from the Compass page 76
    from the Highway page 76
    from the Map page 76
  precoded ~ 118, 144
  remove a waypoint 74
  reversed route 17, 77, 92
  review a ~ 74
  route card 116, 118
  Route function 63
  save a ~ 119
  share a ~ 119
RS232/USB converter cable – *see PC*

S

Satellite Based Augmentation Systems
  10, 12, 13, 16, 20, 37, 124
satellites 10, 11, 18, 37
SBAS – *see Satellite Based
  Augmentation Systems*
screens (**Magellan** refer to 'screens',
  but we call them all 'pages') –
  see pages/screens
SCROLL key – *see keys/buttons*
selective availability 10

SETUP
  **For a list of diagrams illustrating
  GPS setup, see *Index of Diagrams*
  on pages 176–177**

---

setup 42
  barometric altimeter 47
  bearing 44, 45
  coord system 50
  display 42, 44, 51
  distance 43, 50
  electronic compass 46
  elevation 43
  heading 44

information window 48
magnetic variation 44
map datum 43, 50, 140, 143
map screen 45, 51
map settings 43, 50, 143
North reference 42, 44, 50, 140, 142,
  143
orientation 45, 51
personalising your GPS 42, 49, 53
position format 43, 142
setup information 42
speed 43, 50
time 43
  time format 43, 50
  time zone 43, 50
time format 50
units 43
user waypoints 45
Silva 28, 30
software 21, 103
  3D view 103
  aerial view 103
  auto navigation ~ 154, 155
  choice of ~ 105
  finding your way around 111
  fly through 103
  main suppliers 106
  overlay manage 119
  route, track and
    waypoint manager 119
  Save As screen 121
  version 131, 132, 133
street mapping 22
support services 26, 29

T

topographical mapping 22, 23
TracBack 65, 81, 129, 131
  creating & navigating a ~ route 81
track history 54, 64, 65
track log 16, 56, 64, 65, 79, 80, 94, 129
  clear the ~ 80, 94

memory bar 80
saved tracks 56, 79, 94
    find a ~ 95
    Follow Track 95
    navigate a ~ 95
    Reverse Track 95
    save a ~ 119
    share a ~ 119
track route 65
Track Up 39, 45
Tracklogs 107
training courses 29, 30
trip computer 42, 48, 69
    resetting the ~ 69, 83
    trip odometer 83

find a ~ 71, 72, 85
GoTo 62, 72
icon 60
insert a ~ into a route 74, 85
management system 17, 59, 63
marking ~ 59, 70, 84
naming ~ 59, 60, 70
on arrival at ~ 129
proximity alarm 17, 20, 123, 129
replace a ~ 74
websites and support services 26, 109
    FAQs 109
    user forums 28

U

Universal Transverse Mercator (UTM) 3
USB cable – *see PC*
using your GPS abroad 42, 140
    coord system 143
    map datum 140, 143
    map units 140, 143
    North reference 140, 142, 143
    position format 142

W

WAAS – *see Satellite Based
Augmentation Systems*
waypoints 16, 17, 54, 60, 71, 84, 115,
    122
    ~ in a route 117, 124
    ~ in a *TracBack* route 81
    ~ placement 117, 122, 124
    change details of a ~ 74, 85
    change the order of ~ in a route 74
    create new ~ 59, 116
    decision points 117, 124
    default POI file 85, 86
    delete a ~ 72, 74, 86
    edit a ~ 86

INDEX

Index of Diagrams

&GARMIN.

Garmin GPS Setup Procedures:
1 Map Settings, Distance/
Speed & Time 43
2 Bearing & Heading 44
3 Map Screen 45
4 Calibrating the
Electronic Compass 46
5 Calibrating the
Barometric Altimeter 47

A
Amending a Route 74

B
Barometer/Altimeter Page 41

C
Changing the View in
an Information Window 48
Checking the Software Version 132
Clearing the Track Log
Before You Set Off 80
Compass Page 38
Creating & Navigating
a TracBack Route 81
Creating a Route 73

D
Deleting a Route 78

E
Explaining the Keys 35

F
Find Page 57
Finding a Waypoint 71

G
GoTo or Delete a Waypoint 72

H
Highway Page 40

M
Main Data Groups and Functions 57
Main Menu 36
Manually Marking &
Entering a Waypoint 70
Map Page 39

N
Navigating a Route 75

P
Personalising your GPS 49

R
Resetting the Trip Computer 69
Reversing a Route 77

S
Satellite Page 37
Saving a Track Log as a Saved Track 79
Stopping Navigation of a Route 76

T
Trip Computer Page 40

U
Using your GPS Abroad 142

MAGELLAN

Magellan GPS Setup Procedures:
1 Map Settings, Distance/
    Speed &Time 50
2 Map Screen Setup 51

A
Amending a Route 89

C
Checking the Software Version 133
Compass Page 38
Creating a GoTo Route 87
Creating a Route 88

D
Deleting a Route 93

E
Edit or Delete a Waypoint 86
Explaining the Keys 35

F
File Storage System 82
Finding & Navigating a Saved Track 95
Finding a Waypoint 85

I
Information Windows:
    Changing Views 52

M
Main Data Groups and Functions 58
Manually Marking &
    Entering a Waypoint (POI) 84
Map Page 39

N
Navigating a Route 90

P
Personalising your GPS 53
Position Page 41

R
Resetting the Trip Computer 83
Reversing a Route 92

S
Satellite Page 37
Stopping Navigation
    of a (GoTo) Route 91

T
Track Log: Clearing the Active Track/
    Backtracking on Active Track/Saving
    Active Track 94

U
Using your GPS Abroad 143